The Forgotten Man

James Kifer

New Harbor Press / Rapid City, SD

Kifer/New Harbor Press

1601 Mt. Rushmore Rd., Ste 3288
Rapid City, SD 57701

NewHarborPress.com

The Forgotten Man/James Kifer. -- 1st ed.

ISBN 978-1-63357-331-4

Contents

PREFACE

The title speaks of no particular originality. The phrase has been employed in many languages in countless cultures throughout endless generations and ages. In modern times it is perhaps most associated with President Franklin D. Roosevelt in his first campaign for the Presidency in 1932 when he promised that those multitudes of citizens allegedly and seemingly forgotten by huge forces beyond their control, government, business, banks and the generally prominent and powerful would be forgotten no more. In a far different time and in a radically different culture on election night in November 2016 then President-elect Donald J. Trump promised that millions of Americans would be forgotten no more. The extent and depth of the sincerity of both men is an issue of continuing historical and political debate, but only the most rabidly partisan would deny that each President was, at least by his own lights, possessed of some sincerity and feeling for his fellow citizens. Originality, though, was/is not the province of either man, for politicians have harvested great rewards from the wise cultivation of this issue at least since the times of Julius Caesar. The Bible itself opens our eyes to the ubiquity of its usage as a political theme when it tells the story of Absalom's brilliant usage of its appeal when he temporarily usurped power from his father, King David. The historical roster of those who noticed, preached and even pandered to the "forgotten man" is endless, but it is not the subject of our inquiry. More to the point it is the man who is forgotten, and it is to this question we turn our gaze.

But, forgotten by whom? An initial reaction would be tinged with disbelief in thinking of Jesus Christ, of all people, as being among the forgotten. He was the subject and the center of Old Testament prophecy for thousands of years. Upon his arrival he drew the malicious attention of a great king, and was Himself the center and focus of a three-year ministry that excited many to intense love and loyalty and perhaps even more to an intensity of animus and hatred that has never been equaled. He founded a Church that has stood for some two thousand years against all detractors, all persecutors and as Jesus Himself assured that it would withstand the very "gates of hell" itself. Throughout the ages billions, with varying degrees of sincerity, have been His disciples, and many have given their very lives for His name. Conversely in His own day and even today He excites a hatred from many that glows with an unmatched ardor and intensity. Daily, His name is on the lips of multitudes in prayer and in praise, while other multitudes employ His name as a curse. Loved, hated, revered, abhorred, perhaps but forgotten?

To be forgotten one must at some point been recognized and acknowledged, and that certainly is descriptive of the relationship which an untold percentage of the world's population has had with Christ, that is no relationship whatsoever and in an unknown quantity no awareness even. Yet Christians, His professed followers, surely know Him and have forgotten him not. Sadly, though, now as always, His name may be known but His teachings and His character not so much. Really, though, it is to serious and sincere Christians that this small missive is primarily directed. A Christian disciple soon comes to the awareness that we are dealing with two realities when we observe

Christ, two realities that made His character and life unique. These two are that He was both the Son of God and the Son of Man, and it is to the latter we direct the bulk of our attention.

The preface to this study almost demands that many questions be posed. The initial one concerns how any man who was given at least 152 names throughout both the Old and New Testaments be forgotten? That number is only given because a researcher undoubtedly found it to be of manageable size, for our studies will surely discover even more. Each name, from the few offered here, from Light of the World to Advocate, is loaded with innumerable meanings, none of which have fully been discovered and comprehended by any one of us. To realize how even the most sincere and dedicated Christian disciple can forget Christ it is incumbent that periodically we turn introspective and make inquiries and later demands upon our own souls.

For example, have we forgotten that when he tread the land from the shores of Galilee to the streets of Jerusalem that many fell at His feet, wordlessly and even weepingly in awe of being in His presence? Have we forgotten that one day a very sick, worn down and impoverished woman fought her way through the ever-present crowd and lunged at Him, falling to the ground in her certain belief that if she merely touched the hem of His garment she would be healed. Perhaps we have overlooked and let slide down the slopes of our memory that a veteran, hardened Roman centurion, a man accustomed to being obeyed and feared, declared that he knew if Jesus just spoke the word his servant would be healed. Maybe in our thinking and even studying we have forgotten and overlooked that on the Sunday before His crucifixion He was greeted with such popular acclaim that He told His detractors that if His disciples remained silent the stones themselves would shout hosannas of praise?

The most devout, the sincerest and the purest of Christians remain ordinary men and women and succumb to all human infirmities. A serious student will be thorough, yet eventually he will tire of the repetitiveness of certain lessons over and over. The stories of the Old Testament, marvelous and instructive as they are, do not require our daily study and attention. The New Testament teachings of Paul on church organization and church officials require learning but not continual attention. Yet does the sincere Christian ever really tire of the stories of Christ? An old hymn declared the writer's longing to "Tell me the old, old story" of Jesus. Both the child and the mature Christian will find comfort in even the whisper of the names Jesus or Christ. For three years many disciples and His twelve apostles closely adhered to Him, followed His every step, often questioned Him and listened daily to His teachings. The scriptures contain many reactions to the Son of God, but do not look for boredom, as it is absent.

Is it possible that in our worship, sermons, Bible classes and prayers that in too many (but not all) instances the church has strayed from the purity and beauty of the story of Jesus? Has the Christian world (what was once referenced as Christendom) found that radiating from its central core is not Christ but too many tangential, though worthy, concerns about modern church "issues", questions that the world foists upon us and an endless expanding kaleidoscope of interests, questions and subjects that effectively darken our vision of the Light of Christ. Sadly, the heart of the answer to any of these matters which Christians fret and worry is Christ Himself, for He shied not from defining Himself as the sole truth.

One of the most common quotations from the Western literary canon is that "...most men lead lives of quiet desperation." Although Thoreau's moral compass was often askew this brief thought contains more than a gram of truth, especially wherein the spiritual sphere of life is concerned. Although the Bible itself recognizes that the world has always been host to multitudes of the unthinking, "brute beasts" as Paul named them, likely most persons are sentient regarding their ultimate destination. This life is short, and truly as we age, we realize just how short is the journey. So, what comes next? Great hosts believe that the grave is the terminus of existence, and that a void oblivion awaits. Likely some are indifferent to their fate, whatever it may be. The Christian, though, and even many who follow not the name and path of Christ believe that the regard of this existence is an eternal bliss in heaven. How do we attain such, or as the multitude asked the apostle Peter on Pentecost, "what must I do to be saved?" What or who can save me from a feared oblivion, or even worse, punishment? Humanity has sought salvation in so many sources and places, and invariably disappointment is the reward. So where is it found then?

So many good and profitable treasures are often to be found in any search for salvation. The word salvation has always been joined with theology or religion, both profitable studies but neither offers eternal salvation. Even religion in its purest form is lacking any element of salvation, for as James famously defined "pure religion" is their fate, whatever it may be. The Christian, though, and even many who follow not the name and paths of Christ believe that the reward of this existence is an eternal bliss in heaven. How do we attain such, or as the multitude asked the apostle Peter on Pentecost, "What must I do to be saved?" Again, what or who can save me from a feared oblivion, or even worse, punishment? Humanity has sought salvation in so many sources and places, and invariably disappointment is the reward. So where is it found then? Even religion in its purest form is lacking any element of salvation, for as James famously defined "pure religion" is:

"To visit the fatherless and widows in their affliction,
and to keep himself unspotted from the world."

Good, even marvelous, works these are, but we are consistently cautioned that salvation is not found in the performance of good works.

To the Christian the Holy Bible is the Word of God, the very Book of Life, the God-breathed inspiration for its writers and the life's guide for its followers. Further, even apart from religion it is the great and marvelous treasure trove for all literature, especially Western civilization. No person is truly educated without a familiarity with its tragedies, triumphantal tales, the easily recognizable stories of family triumphs and miseries, and most importantly its beautifully and even artfully arranged story of the coming of a Savior, His life, His resurrection and the changes He forever wrought in the universe itself. Boring, dated, passé' and vaguely sinister to the non-believer, to the believer it is a wellspring from which all true wisdom flows. Its deepest study truly may be entrancing, and the depth of its riches has yet to be found. Yet can it save? While a mastery of its knowledge is impressive and admirable the Bible alone has never saved a single soul.

Surely, then, the Church is the great instrument of salvation for its very establishment and story becomes the centerpiece of the New Testament. In its wording it is the "Bride of Christ" and is spoken of as a beautiful creation beautifully clothed and adorned for the time when the Redeemer comes as the Bridegroom. It is the church that is designed as the terrestrial microcosm of Heaven, the arena where the principles of the Sermon on the Mount, the fruit of the spirit such as love, moderation, gentleness and kindness. The church, though, has never saved a single soul. In whatever form, be it the Church established on Pentecost, the Roman Catholic church, or any Protestant group it is incapable of salvation. The Church is the saved. We are left then with only that which remains, our only source and our only possible claim to eternal escape and reward for this life. In the plain, often sung words of a very old hymn:

> "What can wash away my sins. Nothing but the blood
> of Jesus."

It was Christ and He alone who proclaimed that He was "...the Way, the Truth and the Life" and that He was the "...resurrection and the life". Singular and exclusive are these claims, but they are of a splendid, wondrous beauty. We have salvation, we possess the means to Heaven, but perhaps we have overlooked the true path. Many of the New Testament's words are written primarily for the eyes and hearts of Christians, and this small missive seeks to follow the Bible's path. The world has not forgotten Jesus Christ, for how can it forget someone it never knew? It is we, the sincere Christians, flawed and stumbling we may be who can easily overlook and bypass the astonishing character and personality of this Son of Mary and Joseph. In our lives, in our spiritual service, in family and business obligations and even in "church work" the best of Christians may become too entangled and burdened. Good matters and occupations likely they all are, but may we not become like Martha, one of the Savior's dearest and closest friends, whom he had to calm with His voice, and the gentleness of words:

> "Martha, Martha, thou art careful and troubled about
> many things."

It was Martha's younger sister Mary, to whom Jesus pointed, the same Mary who had irritated her older sister Martha by not working "enough":

"But one thing is needful: and Mary hath chosen that good part, which shall not be taken away from her."

It is easier for the modern Christian to slip exclusively into the role of Martha, for we easily forget just who we serve. May we not awkwardly aver that it is often easy to serve while often forgetting the nature of the One we are serving.

Is Christ even worth serving? That is a question unclothed of niceties and on its face actually patently outrageous. It does, though, merit an explanation, for a negative answer is the world's answer, that is, Jesus of Nazareth is not worth studying and certainly not meritorious of worship and should, in fact, be forgotten. Should a man or woman even bother to have a relationship with a man who lived in a remote, backwater land some two thousand years ago? Maybe He should be forgotten, the fate of most humans with the passage of enough time. Yet if we still answer these queries in the positive what sort of relationship are, we to have with this man, ignored by most, misunderstood by many and even at times enigmatic to His closest followers?

In His three-year earthly ministry Jesus was continually besieged by multitudes wishing to see Him, to hear Him, to touch Him, or maybe even to be healed by Him. He was known for the crowds and the variations in people which He drew, but not least of which were small children. In an era and culture which was certainly neither child nor youth oriented the sight of small children huddling around the Savior, clamoring over Him and perhaps impeding the way and the desires of many of His disciples even the apostles became irritated and mildly annoyed at the ruckus and obstruction the children were effecting. The disciples wished to scatter them and not waste the time of Christ, but His response remain shocking:

"Except ye be converted, and become as little children, ye shall not enter into the kingdom of heaven.

Whosoever therefore shall humble himself as this little child, the same is greatest in the kingdom of heaven."

Just as repugnant now are these words to the ears of the world as they were to those who first heard them in the time of Christ. How, though, do they still sound to the religious, those who are His disciples? Do the humbling words of Christ mesh well with the concepts of popes, cardinals, bishops, priests, pastors, reverends, etc., all titles which (let us be honest) are given to elevate the stature of their holders? It is so easy to forget God's words spoken through Peter:

"God resisteth the proud, but giveth grace to the humble."

The character and personality of Jesus Christ was simple yet unfathomable in its depth, but mankind has forgotten this in his ceaseless efforts to complicate Christianity.

A premise of this work is to examine the character and personality of Christ through the prism of just a few of the scriptural names which He was given. Just a brief glance at a few of those titles, though, provides a stark contrast, a true dichotomy, in the manner of which we employ language and the words of God. Jesus has been called the Great Physician, yet he carried no pharmacy of medicines nor did He attend a medical school for a single day. Likewise, He is known as our Advocate, but He never drafted a legal document, never argued a case before a tribunal or court (even His own), never went to law school and certainly never took a bar examination. Jesus was born in a village, grew up in another village and worked at the carpenter's trade, yet He is forever known as the Good Shepherd. It is reasonable to assert representations of Christ as a shepherd than in any other setting, yet for what we can reasonably assume He never tended a single sheep.

He is the King of Kings, though He never sat on a throne, grasped a scepter, held a public office or position or put his name or seal on a public document. He never commanded so much as a single soldier in this world, yet Kings who commanded legions and armies feared His influence and power. With the historic propensity to violence and corruption possessed by so many kings and heads of state it is little wonder that both the beginning and end of His life, earthly rulers quaked in terror. The infamous King Herod the Great so feared this king even as an infant that he hideously ordered the slaughter of untold numbers of infants. As the King of Kings stood before Governor Pilate, who swaggeringly bragged of his life and death power, Christ brought the feared Roman low by showing him that he held no power at all, save from God. Never once on this earth did the true King ever live as a king, yet all shall witness true monarchial glory at the end.

Whether we describe Him by name, by story, by quotation or other means He is the one person of whom we never tire for as perhaps His closest friend, the apostle John who closed His gospel:

> "...Many other things Jesus did, the which, if they should be written everyone, I suppose that even the world itself could not contain the books that should be written."

{ 1 }

LIGHT OF THE WORLD

The birth of Jesus of Nazareth came at the terminus of the greatest public relations failure in the history of the world. Certainly, it had been prophesied many times by many prophets in an abundance of manner, but by the time of the actual birth the last such prophecy was over four centuries earlier. It was spoken of in the earliest chapters of Genesis, reiterated in various words, forms, metaphors and allegories throughout the five books of the Torah and the histories of Israel and Judah and became more specific and recognizable in the Old Testament books of prophecy, from Isaiah, the foremost Messianic prophet to Malachi, the "minor" prophet, whose pen was lain down some four hundred years before the event. So, had God forgotten about, or perhaps had it become less important in His apparent Divine inscrutability?

No, the Creator had not forgotten, but when the publicity began, He found as unlikely heralds as could be located. The announcement of the birth was conveyed by the angel Gabriel to a teenage girl in an obscure village and then to her somewhat older fiancé, a carpenter residing in the same village, one parent just as obscure as the other. The baby's arrival thus came not amidst royal fanfare and acclaim, but rather in an animal feeding trough in an unknown village "in the middle of nowhere."

All events in this present modern age are seemingly public news, and people of all backgrounds and beliefs willingly, nay enthusiastically, participate and persist in publicizing every story, major or minor, and every thought, sublime or mundane, on the internet and its related and supporting devices which instantaneously air and disseminate throughout the world. Publicity and news coverage have been taken from the sole and jealous hands of the professional media and its power and influence given to each of the world's citizenry. Little or no delay now exists in the spread of any news and information, but such was not so in the time of the birth of Jesus. Apart from His very young parents the only ones to whom knowledge of the birth was initially given were a few, humble Judean shepherds, men close to the nadir of the economic and political ladder.

Further, even the old prophecies from the scriptures held only a limited currency. They had been proffered a long time ago by a small, albeit tenacious, group of unpopular men, most of whom were entangled in the immediacy and demands of their missions. It was further a public relations boondoggle because of the locale and the worldly stature of the men who made the prophecies. Judea, Jerusalem, Nazareth and Bethlehem have all become well known to Christians through the ages, but in their day were small and starved of influence. For the greatest fame and splendor, the birth should have occurred in Rome, the city that was reaching its long-standing pinnacles as the greatest in the world. The Savior could have been cuddled in the royal purple of Rome rather than the rough swaddling cloth of Bethlehem.

Viewed in cold, hard logic all of the noted points possess at least a modicum of validity. God, though, has never shown the slightest concern for what is often today called "media savvy" or public relations maneuvers or great and glorious spectacles as defined by humanity. God's essential interest at the dawning of the New Testament was precisely the same as recorded at the beginning of the Old Testament. That is the dissemination of light to clear away and obliterate all darkness. They were two compilations of books written by two groups of men in some instances thousands of years apart in time, but early in each a remarkable similarity of statement is to be noted. God's first recorded words are found in the third verse of Genesis:

> "And God said, Let there by light: and there was light.
> And God saw the light that it was good: and God divided the light from the darkness."

The New Covenant commences with the famous four gospels, but nowhere is the Light more succinctly or beautifully described than in the most personally intense of the four, the Gospel of John, wherein its opening proclaims with exquisite beauty and sadness:

> "In Him was life; and the life was the light of men.
> And the light shineth in darkness; and the darkness comprehended it not."

Certainly the world into which Christ was born benefited from the sun, and the moon and the stars, but it was a dark world into which the masses of its habitants were conceived and born, lived and died without even so much as catching a glimpse of truth and of life, even in a light dimmed by the world. So much do we study and celebrate the birth of Christ, this light come into the world, but rarely do we contemplate the nature of that world.

The famous English theorist and philosopher of the 1600's Thomas Hobbes, once famously wrote that "Life is short, nasty and brutish," and at no time would that have been more distinct than the antiquity into which Jesus came. Among earth's inhabitants only the Jews, circumscribed within the narrow limits of their small land of Judea and supplemented by a relative handful that had been dispersed throughout the ancient world, recognized and worshipped the one true God of the Bible. Even there, the inconsistency and sincerity of that loyalty are matters of historical and Biblical record, yet it was the God Jehovah to whom they pledged loyalty and adherence. Not so the remainder of this world, what we Biblically call the Gentile world and which to this day comprises the bulk of humanity.

The world then was limited by the same confines as it is in the twenty-first century, but for our purposes let the gaze be turned to the world of the Bible. What is easily denominated the Old Testament would was at the birth of Christ remarkably the same as it had been for thousands of years. Splendid though many of its accomplishments were, it was essentially the same as it was in Genesis in the time of Abraham, Isaac and Jacob. It could boast of majestic structures such as the Great Pyramids of Egypt to the magnificent library in Alexandria it was still immersed in the darkness of paganism and heathen gods. The Canaanite practice of child sacrifice had yet to be extinguished and had even spread to other lands. The Canaanites themselves had colonized Phoenicia, north of Judea, and later Carthage on the north African coast, both cultures which painted continually deeper colors of black to deepen the seemingly impenetrable darkness.

In all nations a multiplicity of gods and goddesses, quite often animals partially or fully in human guise was worshiped, and to them were offered sacrifices unceasingly. Yet, the forum, the scene of activity into which the Savior was borne was a Roman world, that along with the Greeks and their efforts for centuries past had given rise to an entirely new civilization, a mode of living that remains, although altered, mutated and hybridized extant yet today – Western Civilization. Surely our ancestors in the West lived not as the eastern world, blinded by paganism and unending bloodlust and warfare. Only a fool could deny the great advances made by these two groups, but their world was likewise darkness. Routinely for centuries Greek parents abandoned newborn babies which they deemed defective or weak, exposing them to the elements and letting them die hideous deaths. The advanced Romans maintained the institution of the "paterfamilias" the male head of the family who was vested with literal life and death power over every member therein. The Romans grew powerful by their mastery over many matters, foremost among them being the ability to march into other lands, slaughter, maim and enslave on a massive scale, and do it all without moral compunction or regret. On we could go about both the Romans and the Greeks, but most germane to the topic is the darkness which enshrouded their religious world.

Both cultures boasted pantheons of gods and goddesses, the detailed study of which has always been a key component of a truly classical education. Their divine numbers were ever increasing, and their narratives and mythologies continually shifting. To fully catalogue such an enormous topic mandates a multi-volume history and analysis, some of which have been written and written brilliantly. For our purposes let the cursory examination focus on the character and ultimate moral effect of the classical deities, those that held sovereignty in the hearts of many, at the time of the birth of Christ. The identity and nature of these gods and goddesses beckons an examination so that the interested student may determine the tone and hue of the world into which its Savior was born.

The pantheon of Greek and Roman gods and goddesses was ever changing, and it is difficult to state what the reigning cultural beliefs and morals were at a given point in time. Each theological system, though, recognized hierarchies of gods, even families of gods and fights and even wars between groups of gods. Generally, the Greeks recognized and worshipped Zeus as their chief god and the Romans a similar deity, whom they named Jupiter. Under their power were multitudes of other divinities, and what we moderns might call "specialty" gods and goddesses. There were gods of the harvest, of wine, banqueting, war, love and even more specifically erotica (from the Greek god Eros). These gods and goddesses in the relevant mythologies seemed to utilize all their time in plottings, conspiracies, wars with other deities, jealousies, passionate love affairs, the more adulterous the better, and every form of wrathful, even inebriated behavior of appalling proportions. It was as if the ancients took the worst (although to them perhaps the most enviable) human qualities and enlarged them to divine proportions, fitted them onto and into them the personalities and characteristics of aberrant, immoral human behavior and then bowed down to these creations as their divine superiors. For the moment suffice it to say that this was/is a distant remove from the Christian Biblical concept of a Trinity of the Father, Son and Holy Spirit.

The feelings and relationships of the Gentile nations to their divinities is incapable of expression in a single sentence; however, it would not be historically unfair and unjust to inventory impressions one obtains from reading their own histories. The classical deities were dark and mysterious, and their ways presumed to be unfathomable and incapable of human comprehension. Their stories, narrative and mythologies are endless litanies of strife, with the gods and goddesses wrathful and violent with each other and especially with mere mortals. The Greek and Roman deities had not only to be continually served but also their desires and whims continually appeased. The Old Testament God is often ridiculously referenced as a God of wrath, vengeance and violence, whereas those titles more properly fit the ancient Gentile deities. Most importantly and even vital to our understanding of the darkness of Gentile religion is that an honest study of Greek and Roman history will find the moral influence of this pantheon of gods and goddesses almost completely absent in the lives of the citizens, great or small. Yes, their histories are replete with tales of ritualistic sacrifices, humbling acts of obeisance and endless tribute to these wrathful beings, yet the lifting of the morals of the people is glaringly absent. Truly then, did the Gentile world dwell in darkness until the coming of the Light, an illumination that took the form of a humble infant born to humble parents.

Our attention must now be directed to the world of the Jews, that tiny precinct of humanity into which Jesus was born. These were the descendants of old Abraham, called out and living apart from the darkness which engulfed the world of the Gentiles. Was the small world into which this baby of Mary and Joseph came a world bathed in sunshine, illuminated by a keen understanding of the true nature of God and His desires for humanity? The religion of the Jews was, in fact, a stark contrast to that of the Gentiles. It was a monotheistic belief, a belief in only one God and that the Jehovah of history. Finally, after multiple centuries of agony the Jews had shaken off the lure and enticement of paganism, and their belief system was the Law of Moses and its moral strictures. Where the Gentile saw an endless array of deities the Jew saw and knew one and one alone, a God who had given them a moral code, a law, a purpose and a direction. Moreover, He had given the Jew His love. The Jews were immensely fortunate to be the chosen and profited from such in numerous ways. They knew the history of God's relationship to mankind and were certainly aware of the grand story of the Hebrew Exodus from Egypt and being delivered the Law, an all-encompassing moral code, from God to Moses on Mt. Sinai. They possessed a rich, detailed history of God's continuous interaction with humanity, and He and His nature were no strangers to the Jews. What was right and what was wrong was not uncharted territory for the Jews, as they knew from childhood the nature and extent of God's will. But does all this mean that the Jews lived and basked in the glow of the brightness of God's light in contract with the bleak and dark world of the Gentiles? In a word, No. No for many reasons. No person who has not known Christ can truly be said to live in the Light, or as the scripture stated "...to pass from darkness into light." Although a substantial number of Jews were faithful adherents to God's Law many more were either religiously "...going through the motions," or open skeptics.

The sad truth, doubtless bitter to God, that at the birth of Christ the Jews, though different, were in no better condition than were the masses of Gentiles who resided in total darkness. The Jewish religious establishment, being the Sadducean priesthood, the Pharisaical teachers and the self-styled all-knowing scribes had draped an ebony canopy over the Jews' religion and moral practices that in its singular way dimmed the light as much as did the Gentile's beliefs. It is sad to say, and we remark with no smugness or glee that religious establishments and hierarchies historically (and certainly Biblically) traditionally bring darkness where there has existed light and place stumbling blocks in the ways of women and men as they seek the path to God. Much of the four gospels is comprised of the accounts of the confrontations of the mature Jesus with these groups and His exposing their teachings as being counter to true religion and a darkening veil over the hearts and lives of the Jews.

Although the Jews certainly practiced no human sacrifice (with one notable exception) in the words of the Savior they "devoured widow's houses," had little or no regard for the poor and unfortunate and desired above all else the praise of others. Their prayers to God passed their lips without ever originating in their hearts. Likely in marital and sexual morals they were more attuned to morality and propriety, but for the Laws of God they began to substitute their own man made traditional teachings and beliefs. To many Judaism had definitely become a commercial religion from which many, not just the clergy, were handsomely profiting. In its own way the Jewish firmament was as dark as the Gentiles' sky. The standard Jewish version of God and religion was one that has not left the world stage today. For worship they had too often substituted ritual and for morality a distorted constricted view of law had come to prominence. They had, in the later words of Christ ignored the "weightier matters of the law, faith, judgment and mercy" and in their stead elevated the importance of ritual. We draw on the common currency of language when we express the sentiment that "Being a Jew was no fun."

Likely at the center, at the very core, of the Jew's troubles was their view of the nature of God as a stern lawgiver, a rigid taskmaster and in the parabolic later words of Christ "...a hard man." The world into which He came was dark and in no small measure because little access to the Light was found.

His only Son, Jesus, was and is God's source of Light for our world, but He was born, reared, grew and became an ordinary man, completely suffused with the faculties and characteristics of other men. One of the elemental questions we will always possess is what did this man, this Light of the World, look like? This is an innate human interest but in our modern very visual age we seem to have an overriding interest in looks. The Light appeared very ordinary with no particular identifying characteristics which would distinguish Him from His contemporaries. A full seven centuries before His birth the prophet Isaiah proclaimed that He would possess no particular physical beauty that would draw men or women to His person. In plain terms, He appeared as an average looking first century Jewish man for which we possess absolutely no contemporary image or description. Moreover, the Jews of Jesus's day were loath to make any sort of physical image or replication of mankind, strictly interpreting the First Commandment. While we have plentiful ancient representations of Julius Caesar, Alexander the Great, the Emperor Augustus and others, we have none of Jesus of Nazareth. So, if he was a prototypical average Jewish man of the first century none did such an average Jewish man appear?

Several years ago, a group of anthropologists and other scientists concerned themselves with the answer to this question. Their detailed research, which included the study of burial sites and human skeletal remains led them to some remarkable, even startling, conclusions. Unsurprisingly they determined that the Jewish people of two thousand years ago were a small people, but the extent of that conclusion is striking to us. The average adult Jewish male was 5 feet 1 inch to 5 feet 3 inches tall and weighed from 115-130 pounds. Although Caucasian, his skin tone was of a hue darker than the typical man of European descent. His eyes were almost certainly brown and his hair thick, coarse, dark brown to black in color and worn fairly long. Except for size these conclusions match remarkably well with they typical historical representation made of Him. Undoubtedly, he was physically strong and likely years work as a carpenter would have added muscles and strength to his physique. All in all, though, we must accept the prophetic descriptions and accept that physically Jesus was an "average man." The Light of the World came as the Son of Man, but an ordinary man whose physical nature would attract no particular attention. The Light of the World did not emanate from the physical, but is source was something far deeper and substantive than the relative triviality of the physical.

The Light of the World was not now just a physical phenomenon, that is the light created by the sun, the burning sphere which God placed in the heavens to illuminate the earth. This Light was not flesh, but was Spirit, a Spirit which burned within Jesus more intensely than any light. The coming of Christ enlightened (and yet still) the world by introducing to humanity an entirely new idea of God. Through this Son of Man God reflected His true nature, long ignored and misunderstood by humanity and showed, not just told, but physically demonstrated the actual, true character of God. Christ forever changed how all creatures were to view the Deity, not as a mean-spirited wrathful god among many gods, but a God who came to serve and sacrifice. From these attitudes and the endlessly told stories of Jesus's life would come a new revelation of God and a new identity for mankind. No more plainly did Christ speak of this new Light than when He told the apostles:

> "The Son of Man came not to be ministered unto, but to minister."

Nowhere did He speak more hauntingly of this ministerial service than when He then added:

> "… and to give His Life a ransom for many."

The gods and goddesses of the world were not ministers, and according to their ancient teachings demanded not just service or servitude but servility. The Gentile gods demanded continual sacrifices, and it was not the Canaanites alone who practiced human sacrifice. Yet, now a Son of God came and offered Himself, not just His spirit alone but His body, as a sacrifice for all humanity. This Deity, come in human form served every moment of His brief life and to the receptive always with moderation, gentleness and kindness.

Jesus Christ revealed the true nature of God and did so in a human form that all may appreciate. He changed not only mankind's concept of God, but also the very relationship of God with each individual man and woman. Without end we may find Biblical examples of the manner in which the Light revealed the true beauty of the real nature and character of God. We would be remiss, though, if attention was not given to the revelatory nature of this Light in another manner. With the coming of Christ, this Light, the darkest corners and most evil caverns of the human heart were and are revealed. The entire nexus between God and man was forever changed, and no longer can any beg excuse for his sins by any ignorance of how to live. Just as the Light shows God's brilliant beauty just as surely does it reveal the depravity of the human heart, in some persons a cavernous abyss of depravity. In those final moments at the Last Supper when Jesus was being engulfed in darkness, He still spoke of the world's rejection of Him:

"If I had not come and spoken unto them, they had
not had sin: but now they have no cloke for their sin."

Upon the coming of this Light, the world was never, can never, be the same again, for its brightness changes everything for all time.

Yet in the main it is certainly not the world that noticed or notices this Light, for with the coming of Christ those that stepped not out from the darkness moved deeper into its followers. It is Christ's followers, the Christians who glory in the Light of the World, a light that began the world and through Christ still shows the way. What an inestimable privilege then that He the true Light is willing to share its glory with us, His followers when He assured us that "…you are the light of the world."

{ 2 }

WONDERFUL

In the beginning only a few understood, and they only dimly. While the birth of the Messiah was not unheralded the fame which He possessed at the start is not the type which is so hungrily, avidly and even viciously sought by many in the world. Instead, though, Jesus possessed what is better termed a "pre-fame" a notoriety as a concept, a promise, an idealization even before He became flesh and blood. His prophecy in the Old Testament fills, well, the Old Testament itself, and that earliest and greatest literary source has been the literary father of endless tomes, treatises and volumes in this prophecy. Now, though, is the time allotted to examine, exclaim and explain the result of this prophecy, the infant, the child borne to the humble Mary and Joseph. If the people had any warning and promise of His coming, what was it and what did they expect?

The first mortal to grasp the wonder that was in the offing, the wondrous marvel of God in the flesh, was a woman named Elisabeth, a mature lady, perhaps even on the verge of old age, who would play no small role herself in the Great Story. She was the spouse of a

righteous but humble priest named Zacharias, who received the shock
of his life while one day in the Temple he was performing his priestly
duties of burning incense. The angel Gabriel informed Zacharias that
his wife would give birth to a child, the forerunner and the harbinger
of the Christ, and his name would be John. Incredulous, the faithful
and virtuous but skeptical priest expressed his doubts of God's will
and ability. His wife Elisabeth, he gasped, was well past child-bearing
age so how could God perform such an impossibility? Struck, angered
and no doubt hurt by Zacharias's response, through Gabriel God assured him that the promise would be fulfilled but also that Zacharias
would be mute, deprived of his ability to speak until the child's birth.

As promised Elisabeth conceived, and once again affirming that
even among the disciples the faith of women is stronger than that
of man, she had a clarity of vision that something that had never before happened was on the cusp of becoming reality. The depth of this
woman's understanding was itself wondrous, and she, even during
pregnancy was not self-absorbed. She knows of an even greater miracle and greater wonder that was close behind, for her very young
cousin Mary was likewise expecting. When an expectant Mary came
to visit her cousin, it was Elisabeth who uttered, even shouted, those
wonderful words which any Christian should joyfully embrace:

"Blessed art thou among women, and blessed is the
fruit of thy womb."

So, John, later to be history's John the Baptist came, and his birth
was followed quickly by that of Jesus of Nazareth. That birth, later
denominated the Christmas story, the old, old story, the most frequently told and celebrated through history. He was a baby, God come
to earth in the form of a man, but an event noted at the time by only
a few. The aged king and murderer, Herod the Great, was terrified

with fear and decreed the baby's death, but there were others, not great in number, but notable nonetheless, those early disciples who recognized that someone special, something marvelous had come in the person of a baby, a baby who was called among many names, "Wonderful," before the humble shepherds in the field had come to view and worship Him.

The infant Jesus was as all infants, doubtless a triad of work, worry and wonder for His parents, but three other of His early acquaintances merit mention and recognition. The first are the mysterious "Wise Men," the Magi from the East who had come hundreds of miles to view the Savior. Whether from Babylon, Arabia or Persia, most likely Persia, they had journeyed from afar to see something truly wonderful. Although not Jews with whom the covenant had been made or the promise given, they recognized that the world had changed permanently and irrevocably. Though they come from afar the next two Biblically recorded encounters are with persons who were blessed with Jesus being brought to them.

In Jerusalem lived one of these, an elderly man of whom we know little save that he was "just and devout" (it is worthy of comment that if a person lives a life and is known by two qualities only, we can aspire for few greater than these). God, as He more often than we admit, evidently took a special liking to this man named Simeon, and that he would not see death until he had first seen the :Lord's Christ." Mary and Joseph, as required by the Law of Moses, took Jesus to the temple, and at last Simeon held Him in his arms, blessed him and announced his own readiness for death with the beauty of this:

> "Lord, now lettest thou thy servant depart in peace, according to thy word.For mine eyes have seen thy salvation."

Not only did Simeon wonder at his reception of this great blessing of not only seeing but holding in his arms the infant Savior, but also did the parents of Christ marvel at this wonder:

> "And Joseph and His mother marveled at those things
> which were spoken of Him."

The wonders did not cease, such wonders that an unknown infant could evoke from an eighty-seven-year-old widow named Anna. She was almost monkish in her service to God, never departing from the Temple and serving God "…with fastings and prayers night and day." No reason exists to believe that the infant Jesus was any more conscious of these early visitors and admirers than would be any other infant, yet they set a pattern that Jesus invariably followed, from birth to death, burial and resurrection. Overwhelmingly was His personal ministry made to the ordinary, common people, not to those of earthly stature and a superabundance of pride. The Gospels reflect that He always accepted (and accepts) any person from any strata of society. It began with obscure parents, humble shepherds and two elderly persons, likely overlooked and forgotten by others. Wonderful He remained and wonderful is our realization that the aged, the obscure and even the downtrodden remained at the center of His ministry. Without excusing or rationalizing anyone's sins or immoral behavior Christ struck a chord with the outcasts and outsiders of society. Even here, though, the wonder of His character and ministry was not limned by any social, economic, or racial group or obviously either gender.

The infant grew "in wisdom and stature and in favor with God and man," and the early impressions He made on many were remarkably renewed. Not just to certain groups or to individuals who society had by passed or discarded but even now to all layers and tiers of society. The infant Savior early in His ministry at the age of thirty delivered

His first lengthy recorded sermon, and His audience consisted of whomever wished to sit upon a hillside listening to Him. He therein delivered the moral truths which fulfilled the message given by God in the Mosaical Law and demonstrated for all time the true deeper nature of Law. In it we find the moral foundation of Christian ethics, and the best, purest examples of the thinking of God and Christ. For two thousand years we have named it the Sermon on the Mount, and to the hearer with an open mind and more importantly an open heart it is as impactful as the day those fortunate Jews heard it in the original voice of the Master. As the great chronicler and apostle Matthew recorded:

> "...the people were astonished at his doctrine: For He taught them as one having authority, and not as the scribes."

In conversational language they were astounded that finally here was a religious teacher who knew what He was talking about, and it was wonderful. For centuries the learned Jewish priests and rabbis, the Sadducees, the Pharisees and the scribes had placed a spiritual strait jacket upon the people. They had been buried under an avalanche of men's laws, customs and traditions and were looked upon by the religious establishment as mere human grist to be ground and milled to their selfish supposedly Divine commandments. Here, though, was a man who taught beautifully, eloquently, yet plainly who understood the battles and burdens of the average person. Here was a teacher, a rabbi, young Himself, who understood the sexual temptations of young men. Though He may have prescribed a remedy not to the favor of all, He knew of what He spoke. This teacher had not been cloistered in a temple and spent His young life debating arcane points of the Law with other religious masters. Rather He had made a living by His hands and the sweat of His brow, and all then or now could immediately grasp that this was a teacher who deeply understood the universal worries of all humanity, not least of which is money and the material condition. As He gently but with the powerful authority of real knowledge, spoke from this small hill all with open hearts understood that this was a teacher who had not only understood but had lived the daily substance of life and knew of the worries and temptations of lust, having enough money to support a family, controlling one's temper and the thous and other elements that compose the grist of life. No wonder they were astonished, and how wonderful it was that this one was different, not a harsh, rigid Pharisee and to many the Messiah Himself.

It was beyond wonderful that a man had come who not only was genuinely interested and attentive to the desperate, the downtrodden and the ill, but one who would actually do something about their maladies and fears. No greater illustration of this can be discovered than the story of Christ's coming as an invited guest to the house of a Pharisee named Simon. While sitting at dinner and conversing with Simon and the other guests a woman appeared in the house, and she had brought an unusual gift, an alabaster box of ointment, a gift which spoke of expense and a beautiful aroma. Standing on no ceremony she interposed on the dinner, dropped to her knees and began to wash the feet of the Savior with her own tears and wiped them with her long, flowing hair and then anointed them with the balm of the fragrant ointment. Simon, the Pharisee, played his role beautifully and with a self-righteousness as deplorable as it was understandable (and relatable) spoke, but only to himself:

> "This man, if He were a prophet, would have known
> who and what manner of woman this is that toucheth
> him, for she is a sinner."

Simon thought He had uncovered Jesus as another fraud, the false Messiah so common at this time, so how startled he must have been when He responded to Simon with a parable that showed Simon that He knew precisely not only the nature and history of the woman but also Simon's accusatory thoughts. Beautifully, wondrously, did Jesus demonstrate that as a great sinner her genuine regret and repentance opened the door to her heart's being abundant with gratitude for her received forgiveness. This teacher was astounding, for while He never for a moment condoned sin He understood sin and the burdens borne by great sinners. It is as wonderful now as it was then that Heaven provides a Savior who lights the path and yet always seeks to help the fallen regain it. This woman seemed to be what Simon thought, a great sinner, but she was self-aware in knowing that this man was not the priesthood, not the doctors and scholars of the Law, nor the scribes, but He was the real thing with an open heart to the penitent. Here, early in His public ministry He established a pattern and a principle, His special concern and compassion for the troubles of women, a compassion that yet remains in full bloom. As His life will fully demonstrate His coming and His ministry to women was seen as something especially wonderful by so many of them. He brought from women a quality and behavior which the thoughtful still recognize today, and that is that in the main women are far more open and expressive of their feelings, emotions, and even fears than are men.

In His early ministry especially, Jesus was besieged and surrounded by crowds, hordes of people, which the Bible consistently references as the "multitudes." In one of those crowds was a woman who in the strictest sense should not have even been in public, much less in the midst of a huge crown. Nonetheless, this woman, was in a pitiable state, possessing a Biblically described malady of "...having an issue of blood twelve years" which had decimated her financially, she having "...spent all her living on physicians." Under the strictures and hygienic standards of the Law of Moses she was ritualistically unclean and not to be a part of public gatherings. This, though, was all subordinate to her desire to be healed, and she revealed an understanding and faith that is awesome yet today. This new man Jesus was different for He was no haughty priest, no intellectual, stern arid teacher far removed from the reality of the problems of men and women. He was so wonderful that she possessed absolute knowledge and faith that she spoke to herself:

"If I may but touch His garment, I shall be whole."

After fighting through a throng of His followers she did just that, brushing the hem of His garment and was made whole. Something about this young man, a stranger to her, and just that, a man, called to her and she readily broke down the rigidity of legal boundaries, the disapproval of the masses and the perceived subordination of women to desperately make her way through the intimidation of a crowd and touch that hem. Not just with this lady's story but with so many others, it is clear that Jesus established a relationship and stature with women that no man heretofore had possessed, and afterwards not even the best of men has attained. As with so many of His characteristics, Jesus was truly sui generis, one of a kind.

Certain persons have often been recognized and even admired for a quality that is variously known as charisma, magnetism or just plain charm. It is the life's blood for entertainers and since Biblical days politicians of all stripes have sought to project it. More than any man who ever lived Jesus of Nazareth possessed it, yet it was not the substance of what other "charismatic" figures own. Jesus was not particularly good looking, had little wealth, no public imagery machine, but He did have His words and His character. Women particularly found

Him appealing. Two already have been noted, but the list of others is lengthy. While passing through Samaria He had a conversation with a woman, who knew Him not, a woman who had come to draw her water supply from a well. In just a few minutes Christ obliterated so many barriers, lines of demarcation that had always been considered natural. Publicly he engaged in conversation with a woman who was not His wife nor kin, and a despised Samaritan as well. Normally, the Jews and Samaritans had neither tolerance nor any dealings with each other. After just a few moments he and the woman spoke in great detail about the woman's personal and marital history, neither exemplary. Whether she was embarrassed or ashamed we cannot say, but she was eager to converse more with this wonderful man who she hailed as a prophet, but of whom He made self-reference as the Messiah.

Not just women with whom He had no prior acquaintance did Jesus relate freely and openly. It is conjecture, but a very strong argument could be fashioned from the Gospels that the two closest friends of Jesus were two young sisters, Mary and Martha, whose company, along with their brother Lazarus, He consistently sought. The friendship was so close that Martha showed no hesitation in speaking sharply to the Savior, chastising Him for effectively "allowing" her younger sister Mary to get away with not doing an adequate amount of work. Jesus took no offense, and seemingly demonstrated good humor at He, the Son of God, being upbraided by His good friend. The moral glory is that the scriptural evidence plentifully demonstrates that women had no difficulty approaching Jesus, talking to Him and engaging His attention in even the most delicate subjects. Such reaction to a man was not found in the Old Testament, and even the seismic changes in society two millennia since have demonstrated no other like Christ, a Master and a Savior who possessed a unique compassion for women, their lives and their difficulties. It is truly wonderful that men even today have such a role model, such an exemplar, for dealing with women.

This Son of Mary and Joseph, the oldest sibling in a large family, Himself unmarried and childless has still captured the attentions and imaginations of all children throughout the ages. As the old song refrain goes, "...red, or yellow, black or white, they are precious in His sight," but this is more than just the quaint lyrics from a child's Sunday School lesson. In His frequent dealings with children, Jesus demonstrated at least two great moral teachings, one of which is more studied, and it is to the familiar one to which we first turn.

Children flocked repeatedly to Jesus, and this fact caused more than a little chagrin and annoyance not to Christ's enemies but to His disciples. Doubtless He would appear, and many children in the crowd would head straight for this special man. This was a stream of youthful, childhood exuberance but also came untold numbers of children, even babies, hurt, sick, perhaps even deformed, brought to Him by their parents. The imagery of Jesus surrounded by children, setting them on His lap is an artistic genre' in and of itself, as countless paintings, statues and other works have depicted this through the centuries. Yet many of His disciples believed that Jesus had many other matters that needed His attention and the more important adults upon whom He should give His attention. They attempted to remove the pesky little ones, shoo them off and get down to the business of "serious" religion. Unsurprisingly, Christ saw the matter differently, and how wonderful it has been for Christianity that He did. In a famous passage He admonished the disciples:

> "Suffer the little children to come unto me, and forbid them not; for of such is the Kingdom of God. Verily I say unto you, Whosoever shall not receive

the Kingdom of God as a little child, he shall not enter therein."

Is this a clarion call to childishness? Is it to be argued that the true path of Christianity is a childish playground of immature behavior, silliness and short-sightedness? We must issue a cliché and emphatically state that nothing could be further from the truth. Every principle, iota, minutia and spark in Biblical moral teaching is an arrow directing the disciple in his growth to real Christian maturity. It is the "childlike" not the childish which God seeks. The childlike is open and loving, wanting to accept and knowing that something and someone is better than herself. The childlike disciple, no matter what the years, the troubles, travails, the knowledge, the experience still gets excited at the very thought of the Savior. The health of the aging disciple may be fading, the strength slipping and the joints and sinews deteriorating, but upon pondering the wonderful image of the Savior, he still dreams of leaping into His arms and being caressed as a child. That is the childlike spirit of some of the toughest men who ever lived, the names of such as Peter, Paul, John and Stephen whose legacies cascade before us. their hearts, though, were the substance of what Christ desired, the childlike non-cynical and perhaps, most importantly, the spirit which pride had been subordinated to Christ.

To the sincere disciple and perhaps even to a favor-minded non-believer the necessity of a childlike spirit may be easily harvested from Christ's message. Another, though, every bit as important as this, is easily and often overlooked. The observer here sees a problem which still onerously besets mankind yet today, and that is the desire of many, some with good intentions and others with but little thought, to limit access to God. It is only fair to remark that the Old scriptures reflect that after the Fall only a limited number of persons were given direct access to God. In the olden, ancient days the Almighty mainly expressed His will be speaking directly to the patriarchs, men such as Abraham, Isaac, and Jacob and then such as Moses, the judges and the prophets. Under the Mosaical Law only the high priest could offer atonement for the people's sins, and then only once a year in a very elaborate liturgical ritual. By the time of Christ's ministry, the priesthood, scribes and Pharisees felt that they had been granted a special patent on understanding God, and the supplicant sinner filtered his dealings with the Divine thought the prism of their approval. Nor did it cease with the ending of New Testament days, for what was once commonly called Christendom has suffered this plague for two thousand years.

Soon after the Apostolic Age the seeds of clerisy and clerical exclusivity began to be planted. Eventually it was ordained and with the haughtiest presumption that only clerics could understand the Will of God, and they would dispense it in carefully measured amounts to the "ignorant' laity. So, embedded in the catechism of Roman Catholicism in the late Middle Ages was it that even to possess a copy of the scriptures in the language of the people was a capital offense. It was the guarded preserve of bishops, priests, cardinals and popes. Even now a phrase has made its intrusive way into our language, and that is the great beneficence of being "…granted an audience with the Pope."

Neither did many of the Protestant denominations and sects which followed in the wake of the Reformation entirely eschew this almost "bureaucratic" vision of access to God and His desires. Depending upon the organization many are top heavy with their conventions, associations, synods and in the matter of individuals, priests, pastors, reverends and proceeding almost ad infinitum. Yet, what did the wonderful Savior say of the children, "Let them come unto Me." Multitudes whose hearts are directed towards the Light and towards

God have been encumbered and laden with every conceivable religious doctrine, catechism and creed, all the more sadly, when Christ simply and beckoningly pleaded"

"Come unto Me, all ye that labor and are heavy laden, and I will give you rest. For My yoke is easy, and my burden is light."

No man, woman, church, council, association, priest, pope or pastor stands between the Christian and God. Nobody, save one, Jesus Christ Himself, making intercession for the believer. Unchecked, without shame, without bowing the knee to any graven image or to any man, the Christian revels in true freedom and liberty in Christ. The Christian's lips and heart may open wide without requiring the approval of anyone, other than the impulsion of his own heart to His Creator. How wonderful it is that the Christian has a Father and His Son, the Advocate who encourages His children to:

"...come boldly unto the throne of grace, that we may obtain mercy, and find grace in time of need."

{ 3 }

COUNSELLOR

John Donne was a remarkably accomplished man. Born in England in the year 1572 he grew up in what was contemporarily termed a "recusant" household, which meant that his family were Roman Catholics in a period when the open practice of that religion was illegal. His great natural abilities were enhanced by a fine education at those twin pillars of English education, Oxford and Cambridge Universities. As a young man he gradually abandoned Catholicism and became a cleric in the favored, established Church of England and wrote extensively of what he perceived as the true Christian religion. Adding to his resume he became a member of Parliament and was a player on the age's political stage. It is for his poetry, though, that John Donne is best remembered. He is considered the greatest poet of the English metaphysical poets and generally one of the great poets in the English language. As varied and impressive were his accomplishments Donne is best known for a single verse of poetry that is often quoted yet today:

"No man is an island entire of itself; every man is a part of the continent, a piece of the main. Any man's death diminishes me, because I am involved in all mankind."

The depth and the wisdom of Donne's lines has been proven and continues to be demonstrated each day continuing into the very different age in which we live.

As astute and gifted with a literary brilliance as was Donne his words were uttered sixteen centuries prior by a man with whom Donne was surely familiar. In writing his great letter to the Romans the apostle Paul remarked:

"For none of us liveth to himself, and no man dieth to himself.

For whether we live, we live unto the Lord; and whether we die, we die unto the Lord;

whether we live therefore, or die, we are the Lord's."

Each of these two men, both possessing an intellectual grandeur and one inspired in these short statements recognize a problem that has plagued humanity from the outset, that being the feeling of isolation, even more commonly termed loneliness. The Creator first identified this upon fashioning Adam from the dust of the earth. His awareness led to His remark that "It is not good that man should be alone," and thus created woman. The long human story is a tale of tens of billions of persons inhabiting our small world, of untold marriages, births, friendships, alliances and such, yet it requires no particular insight to observe that even so the percentage of these persons throughout this world who suffer the pains of isolation and the shadows of lonely days and nights is as great, or maybe even greater, than ever. Obviously, men and women need more than themselves, no matter now true the friendship or deep and passionate the love between man and woman, it can never dispel the dread of isolation and of loneliness.

All need someone with whom to talk, to share pleasantries, intimacies and problems, and the decent-hearted all wish to help one another. In the modernity of the twenty-first century we find that these needs have burgeoned into a huge industry, even a doctrine and an inveterate need to seek continual help from someone. The modern, western world is a gargantuan sized therapeutic clinic with psychiatrists, psychologists, counselors, life coaches, doctors and assorted therapists ad infinitum there to guide the patient through the thickets of isolation and depression. All have a place, and the right counseling and counsellors have done many persons great good, helping with difficult life problems. None is a panacea, however, and even the best has limited utilitarian applicability. One counselor, though, predates them all, the man foretold to be called "wonderful, counsellor," Jesus Christ Himself.

As in every other facet of His personality and character this therapist is different, radically different, then all the others. The earthly life of Jesus of Nazareth was of a short span, but it is the greatest proof ever offered that wisdom does not necessarily come with age nor is powerful human insight denied to the young. Jesus had grown up, not necessarily in poverty, but in circumstances which demanded hard work, marked by abundant physical labor by everyone in the family. His eyes had seen, and His heart had absorbed that just life itself was often a burden, on both the good and the bad, on both the faithful and the irreverent. He saw that just everyday living, even when a person was carrying no special problems could be a …burden. How often Christ spoke of burdens, and how often He taught and demonstrated that at the heart of His religion, at the core of Christianity, was the recognition that all men and women bore great burdens. His knowledge and His religion, though, was more than just an awareness of burdens but an opening of a path down which the burdens would not necessarily disappear, but would be lessened and rendered easier to bear. Not in the abstract, though, did Jesus teach, for He was perhaps the least theoretical teacher who ever spoke. He dealt in real situations, real persons, real burdens and real solutions. His counsel was never the counsel of despair nor was it the counsel of perfection. Christ knew that in this fallen world humanity would always be burdened. To the very core of His existence He knew this for ultimately, He would bear more burdens than any soul who ever lived. His counsel, though, was not theological or ethereal as was that of His day's religious establishment, but rather it confronted forcefully the everyday burdens, even the mundane and the tedious of ordinary life. These are the burdens immediately recognized by either a first century Judean or a twenty-first century modern.

One day Jesus had been invited to dinner at the home of perhaps His closest personal friends, two sisters Martha and Mary and their brother Lazarus. In one of the most familiar New Testament narratives we find Martha, a super hostess, completely in charge of the dinner, completely in charge of the household and completely spent and frazzled from the burdens of preparing a feast for the Son of God. Scurrying about, likely about to drop on her feet she notes the apparent inactivity of her younger sister Mary, who is idling and doing nothing more than sitting at the feet of Jesus, listening to Him teach. It is all too much for Martha, and her temper breaks, yet she does not snap at her sister but rather at the honored guest, the Son of God Himself. "Cumbered about with much serving" she levels her fire at Jesus:

"Lord, dost thou not care that my sister hath left me
to serve alone? Bid her therefore that she help me."

Revealing the closeness of His friendship with Martha and ignoring her chastisement, likely with a sympathetic smile He responds:

"Martha, Martha, thou art careful and troubled about
many things…"

Such a rejoinder reveals an understanding of the human condition
that is Divine. Gently He effectively counsels her to calm down and
not get so worked up. These are plain words that bespeak an understanding of a human frailty as common, perhaps more so, today as it
was then. Christ saw that Martha was doling what many always have
done, in overburdening herself. Nowhere in the Bible are laziness and
sloth receptors of anything but condemnation, but often the best counsel is simply to slow down, as Christ continued:

"But one thing is needful: and Mary hath chosen that
good part, which shall not be taken from her."

Of course, Jesus was appreciative of Martha's efforts, but it is impossible to imagine Christ being dissatisfied with any meal placed
before Him. The temporal is important, but the spiritual as chosen by
Mary is vital. Good food satisfies hunger, but the words of Christ ease
burdens.

Unlike any before Him and to a degree none other who followed
ever reached Christ understood and proclaimed that religion itself had
become a burden. As shocking as it may be to read such a statement
it is more so to write it. Both pale, though, almost to triviality when
we realize that a key theme in Jesus's ministry was that religion itself

had become an unbearable burden, not just a burden, but one that was breaking its adherents. How many people must have not only breathed sighs of relief but also shouted silent hosannas of joy when Christ made such remarks of the scribes and Pharisees:

> "For they bind heavy burdens and grievous to be borne, and lay them on men's shoulders; but they themselves will not move them with one of their fingers."

Grievous burdens? In this true religion? The men and women Christ mingled and mixed with, taught and of whom He made friends had all been reared under the God-ordained Law of Moses. That Law was both moral and administrative in nature, moral in that it codified the laws of which mankind was really already aware. A person did not murder, steal, lie, or commit blasphemy, and yes it certainly added rules and regulations regarding the manner in which the Israelites were to live. It regulated property, commerce, family relations and the manner in which a person was to worship God. Certainly, though, it was bearable and meant to guide the people in its fulfillment in the person of Jesus Christ. Through the centuries, though, the Jewish religious hierarchy had undergone a transformation. The priesthood, the scribes and the sects of the Sadducees and Pharisees were comparatively few in number, but their grip on power and the regulation of even the minutia of human behavior was constantly becoming more absolute. They astutely, instinctively and rightfully recognized that their enemy in these endeavors, a man and a teacher unlike any they had seen before was this itinerant young carpenter from the backwater of Galilee. Not only must He be opposed, but ultimately destroyed, for He taught such outrage as "I am meek and lowly" and true religion consisted not in how many burdens under which the people would groan, but rather in such contemptible qualities as humility, modesty, meekness and gentility. When the seekers of truth heard His voice how much could they feel those massive, oppressive burdens of "Touch not, taste not, handle not" being gently but firmly lifted from their backs and shoulders when they heard such of His words as:

> "Beware ye of the leaven of the Pharisees, which is hypocrisy."

How their heart was abound in joy when they saw that at last someone had arrived with true religious counsel, a man who would stand without fear against the religious establishment of the day. He simply had to be destroyed.

The greatest synopsis of true religious counsel and the manner in which humanity can best bear its burdens undoubtedly is found in those three short chapters in Matthew of the greatest and most famous lesson ever delivered, what is forever known as the Sermon on the Mount. Christ knew and taught that the great burden was not political, not religious oppression or persecution, poverty labor or any other such factor. He knew that the greatest burden carried by all men and women is sin, the true burden which destroys the soul and destroys without feeling or any mercy whatsoever. In these few words the Son of God identified the problems that evolve into life destructive, joy robbing and soul crushing sins. He spoke with a lucidity, with a beautiful artistry of words that identified the commonality of burdens shared equally in the first as in the twenty-first century. He counseled against our letting any disagreement with a brother or sister become so severe that it leads us into a sinful antagonism which destroys the relationship.

Christ spoke on topics of which many then and even now are reluctant to speak. A man's desire for a woman and his passion for her is generally presumed to be one of life's greatest, at times the greatest, joy for a man. Yet Christ was so bold as to starkly speak of the realization that sexual desire itself can be a burden. He counseled that a man (or woman) should not begin the lust for another's spouse which remains one of the great wholesale destroyers not only of marriages, but of souls. Do not even begin the desire, which will soon turn to lust, and perhaps then consummation and the obliteration of marriages and souls. In plain language, Christ understood men.

He understood that we live by the "sweat of our brow," have to labor for our sustenance and continually worry about money and our material condition. Christ had worked for His living and knew that this was a universal concern for all humanity, everywhere and at any time, and that it, too, was a universal concern of God. He was able to offer words of assurance and counsel that "...your Heavenly Father knoweth that ye have need of these things." Then, in that phrase that projects the theme of the greatest of all speeches He adds:

> "But seek ye first the kingdom of God, and His righteousness; and all these things shall be added unto you."

Only a Counselor named Christ can assure His disciples with certainty that provision will always be made for them.

A professional counselor, if sincere, qualified and competent is a person to be respected and even admired. Many have gone and continue to avail themselves of their professional services and doubtless in an abundance of instances have been well served. Our vast telecommunications network lists an almost endless array of counsellors and therapists who offer their services to the public. They charge (quite rightly) for these professional services and like most will often even solicit for business. Our Divine Counselor, though, has always gone by a different business plan, for He is the Counselor who not only seeks clients but begs and pleads for them. In a solicitation packed with as much emotion as any scripture, shortly before His Passion He overlooked the City of David and lamented:

> "O Jerusalem, Jerusalem, thou that killest the proph-
> ets, and stoned them which are sent unto thee how of-
> ten would I have gathered thy children together, even
> as a hen gathereth her chickens under her wings, and
> ye would not."

So much of the Counselor's nature and emotions are here expressed, commencing with the sorrowful recognition that the people not only scorn His services but have a long history of actively persecuting the God who seeks to help them. Written to first century Jerusalem this is easily translatable to all nations at all times.

Truly it was also remarkable that a young man such as Jesus hesitated not in utilizing a feminine image to express His overwhelming love, that of the purest, most exemplary earthly love, that of a mother for her children. The heartbreak of Christ's expression of unrequited love is more than palpable when He employs those simple words "... and ye would not." An old adage, in variant words, expresses the folly of "killing the messenger" for having delivered a message the hearer did not wish to receive. This applies to Christ and humanity, but its limitations are obvious. Christ came not with a bad message, but a wonderful message, the greatest the world has ever heard, but His message was not in any book, any Law and could not be confined to any one sermon. The message and the messenger were and are one. Christ is both, and He was crucified by the same humanity that spat at Him and scorned His counsel.

Surely a good professional counselor seeks a rapport, a type of friendship, even a bond with the patient, yet Christ, the Counselor, seeks more. Earlier in His ministry He looked out upon a multitude of thousands, not Jews, not Gentiles but rather:

> "(H)e came out, saw much people, and was moved
> with compassion towards them, because they were as
> sheep not having a shepherd."

No decent counselor with any degree of mental and emotional balance would offer himself as the answer to his patients' problems. Yet, Christ is different, and He did in so many ways, none more succinctly than when He stated that "I am the Way, the Truth, and the Life." If we view this man as just that, a man, we might conclude that this person is an egocentric maniac, offering himself as the solution to all problems. Yet, He is man and God, and as with all things Christ made no bare statements without providing reason and guidance.

Note was earlier made that Christ pleaded and begged for all to become His patients, and He implored each member of humanity to case burdens upon Him, "For my yoke is easy, and my burden is light." One need never have read a history book, a newspaper, a psychology or psychiatric text, or viewed the internet to know that all men and women always have and in this temporal sphere always will bear burdens. Burdens and life often are two words in a balanced equation. As Jesus grew and finally matured as a man He knew of burdens and knew that this would be the lot of humanity until Judgment. His mission was to save each soul but also to lighten, not always remove, but to lighten and make easier to bear the burdens which a person bears. Not only is Christ the wisest of Counselors but also is He the truest of Counselors. Nowhere in either Testament are the disciples promised a burden free life. In fact, the closest and most famous of His followers, were given the following promise:

> "They shall put you out of the synagogues: yea, the time cometh, that whosoever killeth you will think that he doeth God service."

What the Great Counselor knew is that the Christian's life would contain much the same substance as the life of the non-believer. She would suffer the physical ailments and maladies, financial worries, fatigue, fear, depression and on it goes. What He counsels, though, is that in the fiercest of life's battles He will not abandon us in the midst of the fight. Even in the middle of His own problems, during His Passion, whenever the horror of crucifixion and His own death loomed Christ never ceased speaking of Heaven, a place where "burden" is unknown, a forgotten relic of earth's history.

His great counsel was to remember that with Him the greatest burdens of life are bearable and ultimately will be extinguished. Even more strongly and more importantly, however, did He teach that the greatest of all burdens was a load none of us could bear and could only be removed by His sacrifice. Perhaps no more succinctly nor starkly did He express the duality of these burdens than when He cautioned:

> "Be not afraid of them that kill the body, and after that have no more than they can do.
>
> But I will forewarn you whom ye shall fear: Fear him, which after he hath killed hath power to cast into hell; yea, I say unto you, Fear him."

Christ knew that this life's burdens could be great, that just the daily mundane existence of life has the potential to wear the body, the mind and even the soul. The Counselor offers Himself as the counsel and the remedy for each. With Christ, even at its harshest this temporal life is bearable, but with Him the eternal is endlessly perfect.

Before this essay concludes let us examine in greater depth a phrase which was quoted earlier and here is offered in its entirety:

"Come, unto me, all ye that labor and are heavy laden, and I will give you rest.

Take my yoke upon you, and learn of me; for I am meek and lowly in heart: and ye shall find rest unto your souls.

For my yoke is easy, and my burden is light."

Has this world ever been the home to a single human being who was not heavy laden? That is a given fact and common to the human experience. Momentarily let our fixation be on that last phrase of the easy yoke and the light burden. To a primitive agricultural society, the light yoke was a concept easily grasped, for what good farmer would desire to overly strain the animals who assist him in making his living. We must accept Christ at face value where he employs that words "easy" and "light" and not distort their meaning to be "comparatively" light and easy. It was deep in the Old Testament book of Proverbs where God related that "the way of the transgressor is hard," and the relief of difficulties is to be found in His Son.

Throughout the short four-gospel biography of Christ it is consistently seen that the anger of Jesus was not easily aroused, yet what did kindle His fury was the oppression of anyone, especially the faithful, in the name of religion, in the name of God. The centerpiece in our recollection of this side of Christ's nature is likely the famous scene in the Temple where the Son of God is so outraged with the extortion of the moneychangers and the desecration of His Father's house that He drives them out with a whip. The abuse He absorbed from His many detractors over a three-year ministry was rarely answered by Him other than through demonstration of good works and reason. Finally, though, the Son of Man responded to three years of verbal abuse, scorn and mockery when at the end He pivoted and excoriated His critics for what He knew them to be, hypocrites. He so joined the words "scribes and Pharisees" with "hypocrites" and forever will they bear that shame. Christ verbally lashed them for a sham religion that "looked good" and provided self-glorification to its leaders, but in reality, was a dark contrast to its burdened practitioners. Nothing raised His Divine ire and even harshness when He saw that the Laws of God had been so distorted and perverted that they elevated the trivial and ignored the substantial. He counseled that their brand of religion oppressed and suffocated the people, a people He viewed with tenderness, souls that need understanding and inspiration, not more burdens. Yet He brazenly through in their faces what was to them an acid, His accusation and knowledge that rather than God's favored few they were His enemies. They "...devour(ed) widows' houses and for a pretense made long prayer."

This was the nature of religious and spiritual leadership under which God's disciples gasped for breath. The contrast with the humble Jesus of Nazareth is as striking as anything this world has seen. Did the typical Jewish disciple believe that he could go to such men, such hardened scholars and priests and receive understanding and wise counsel. It is hardly likely. The understanding, the fulfillment of the Law and the tenets of true religion emanated from the teacher who issued the Sermon on the Mount, who himself had already lived much of life, a true Counselor who gives His disciples eternal assurance that:

> "I am with you always, even unto the end of the world."

{ 4 }

PRINCE OF PEACE

Everyone desires peace, or at least that is what we have been told. Especially in modern, developed countries the desire for peace, and its essentiality is taken as a sine qua non for a decent society and a livable individual life. The history of mankind is the history of warfare, the presumed opposite of peace, and it was the great subject of our present interest who once remarked that we shall always "…hear of wars and rumors of wars."

Although the warrior ethos and the warrior himself has long been the subject of respect, even reverence, in most cultures, including our own, the popular cultural and artistic spheres swing the pendulum overwhelmingly to the side of peace. During the most tumultuous and culturally significant decade in modern American history, the 1960's, the outcry for peace became cacophonous until in a strange irony the demand for peace itself almost became a war chant. those of a certain age remember yet the endless din of demands of such popular songs as "What the World Needs Now is Love," "Where Have All the Flowers Gone" and "Give Peace a Chance," all with noble, but at times treacly sentiments. Underlying the noise of political and cultural debate, though, is the centrality of truth that peace is good. Only a megalomaniacal aggressor or a fool desires war. It is an unspoken assumption that war is the opposite of peace, yet is this always true? Is the tranquility of a pastoral scene the opposite of a blood-stained humanity mangling battlefield? In certain very real ways, the answer is a resounding yes, for almost all wars are fought so that they may themselves be ended and a new age of peace appear. Humanity will always fight their wars, large and small, they will be observed, written about, lamented and each ended. Yet is the peace that follows the peace of which God spoke and His Son, the Prince of Peace, taught? To be designated a "prince" is special, for the prince is the son of a king, the man closest to the monarch and the king's right hand. He must know at least something of the substance in the title by which He is ennobled.

As with most matters it is usually best and most instructive to begin at the beginning. a very important portion of the birth and nativity of Jesus is what today would be known as a birth announcement. We may safely assume that His parents, Mary and Joseph, did not send out glossy birth announcements on embossed stationery announcing His birth. Paper is temporal, easily lost and destroyed, but His birth was announced on high:

> "...A multitude of the angels praised God, saying
> Glory to God in the highest, and on earth peace, good
> will toward men."

Jesus, the Son of God and the Son of Man, came to earth as the Great Fulfillment, and He simultaneously flawlessly performed many roles, one of which was as ambassador to the world, a place He never claimed as His home. This earth already had its prince, another "forgotten" man and the prince of a world in which Christ's close friend and apostle described:

"And the light shineth in darkness; and the darkness comprehended it not."

Here is one of whom Christ knew intimately, for this prince profits greatly from the fact that "...men love darkness rather than life, because their deeds were evil." In the words of Christ Himself he is the "prince of this world" and to whom the apostle Paul gave the appellation, the prince of darkness, Satan himself. This is a being with whom peace has never in any form or fashion been associated. Our Prince of Peace, the tender, loving humble Jesus came to destroy, to crush, this prince, and Christ never hesitated in admitting so. The Prince of Peace Himself, a warrior, a destroyer? How can this be so? The answer must lie in the Divine definition of peace for as God has always reminded His creation the thoughts of God are not those of man.

The son of God as an infant entered into a world in which the Prince of Darkness held sway, and had almost everything going his way, the way to perdition. Without the influence of God in the hearts of men and women, Satan knew then, that he held sway, and that he, not God, reigned supreme. The magnificent writer and Christian apologist, C. S. Lewis, brilliantly and succinctly summarized the state of the world then and now when he observed that God's disciples live in "enemy occupied territory." Christ came into this world as a baby and His mission was to redeem the most valuable commodity this world contained, humanity itself, from the seemingly unbreakable clutches of Satan. In effect the proper question is whether the Prince of Peace was committed to crushing the Prince of Darkness with a war. The correct answer to this question is yes, a seeming incongruity and the greatest of ironies is it that the Prince of Peace had come to wage a war. It is Christ Himself who seemed to deepen this incongruity with a statement, well know and oft quoted, that appears in direct contradiction:

> "Think not that I am come to send peace on earth: I came not to send peace, but a sword.
>
> For I am come to set a man at variance with his father, and the daughter against her mother, and the daughter in law against her mother in law."

This, from the man called by the prophet Isaiah the "Prince of Peace." Much of this discussion must be devoted to the logical and reasonable questions of whether Christ came to cause division or reconciliation and just as important what did the heavenly herald mean when he announced the coming of peace with the birth of Christ.

Let us examine the second inquiry first to determine with greater precision the divine definition of peace, a definition contrasting with that of the world's answer, which is essentially the absence of war. Most certainly, we may be assured that our Creator detests earthly war, strife between nations, groups, families and individuals. The humanity which He fashioned for His love and glory gives Him no pleasure when he sees people fall upon each other as jackals and vultures. But if the absence of war is a good thing (and most certainly it is) it does not necessarily bring peace. A great Roman historian famously said of his fellow Romans as they conquered by the sword:

> "They make a desert, and call it peace."

Surely the peace of Christ is more meaningful and of deeper substance than this. this great ancient observation comes very close to the purest understanding of peace being the absence of war. All of the teachings of Jesus direct us to a deeper, a more profound understanding. To Christ and His followers, the Christians, the opposite of peace is not war, but rather the opposite of peace is fear. How frequent, how abundantly often, did the Prince of Peace begin His teaching with those his blessed words "Fear not." Jesus, the Son of Mary and Joseph, was a man who understood that all men and women live in fear. Long before the famous American Thoreau wrote that "Most men live lives of quiet desperation," Christ was fully aware of such fear, and His awareness went to the very core of His Divine Being. Read through the most famous on morality ever delivered, the Sermon on the Mount, and it will be found the intimate awareness of humanity's everyday fears. In this short message alone knew and spoke of man's fears of letting his anger lead to violence, of his desire leading to lust and adultery and of his fears that the sincere life of being virtuous, of doing good, would eventually break him down. Christ with an intimacy that is astonishing penetrated the human heart and saw that all have material fears, the terror a man can have when he sees no possible economic route to providing for his family, the fears of aging and the breakdown of health. He perceived them all and offered remedies and assurances of what the days' religious teachers were bereft. When the people of His day listened to the priesthood, the scribes and the Pharisees they feared that they would be reminded of obligations and tasks yet to perform, of details overlooked and of greater burdens to bear. When Jesus of Nazareth spoke, they could sense something never before presented to them, the easing of burdens, the exaltation of the true character of God, of faith, mercy and justice, and of a man who understood them. Religion, true religion was now being offered and extolled and the clouds of fear were parting. They were "...

57

astonished at His teaching, for He taught them as one having authority, and not as the scribes." Are not matters still the same?

The Prince of Peace had come to reconcile each and every soul to God, and to remove a certain type of fear that had been instilled into them. Correctly mankind is to "Fear God and keep His commandments," but not with the fear of God's constant wrath. This is a fear which is difficult to reconcile wit God's true character. This is the misunderstood nature of God which ran rampant among the Jews at the time of Christ's coming, and which He illustrated so well in one of His most famous stories, the Parable of the Talents. There the slothful servant essentially did nothing with his faith and his life for he knew that his master, parabolically God the Father, a "hard" man, a vengeful tyrant who sought to punish with severity the slightest of infractions. This was the idea of God to many of the Pharisees, an idea driven into the people with an ever-steady drumbeat. How could or can any man or woman have peace with such an idea of God, a divinity with a watchful, vigilant eye of love and protection but of draconian severity, not just willing but seemingly even eager to punish even the most serious disciple for the slightest offense.

The Prince of Peace came not as a revolutionary religious teacher obsessed, as revolutionaries are wont to be, with overturning any existing order. His self-annointed purpose was not to destroy the Law but to "fulfill" it. He came not to increase burdens but rather to lighten them. As Christ so ably identified the flaws and falsehoods of the existing dominant religious order, He likewise offered the alternative, that being the path of true peace, with Himself as the Prince. Most certainly, even emphatically, He proposed no system of religious works as the sure path to Heaven. Even today, when a person becomes a Christian the well-meaning words of well-meaning Christians are often heard and heard resoundingly in statements such as "Now the real work begins" or "We will put you to work." This doctrine is as untrue to Christ and the teachings of the New Testament as any falsity that could be expounded. the clear, consistent, even precise teaching of Christ and His apostles is that not only has the performance of good works failed to save a single human soul such an efficacy is an impossibility. When a Christian burdens other Christians, especially the "babes in Christ" that Christian is acting not as the purveyor of the teachings of the Prince of Peace but rather in the spirit (dare we say it) of Phariseeism. True religion, true Christianity, is evidenced partly by works, but they are the works of desires which arise in the individual Christian's heart. To employ the words of the apostle Peter they are "the answer of a good conscience towards God," not the result of the external imposition of commands, dictates and heavy-handed persuasion which most often prepare the conscience as a seedbed of resentment and unnecessary guilt. Truly Christ was a Prince for He knew that peace came from within, not from external command. The humblest, meekest Christian, though, is entitled to an answer from His Prince to the question of how exactly is the internal peace of which you, Christ, speak to be found.

No Christian who poses these questions should ever feel alone, for they were prominent among the disciples from the beginning. Moreover, Jesus recognized that even the most famed and trusted of His disciples would be troubled by such a question. Those, of course, were the twelve apostles, personally chosen by Christ and later recognized to be, along with the earlier prophets, the very "foundation" of the Church. The apogee of Christ's teachings on peace and the passages in which He most reveals Himself as both the Son of God and the Son of Man, is found in the gospel account of John, the account wherein the nature of peace and the inner beauty of Christ is most revealed. Only a few short hours before His arrest, trial and crucifixion

Christ met with His apostles in the celebrated "upper room" and there began a discussion, a study, a lesson, a dialogue, an event by any name which is the most revelatory in all history of intense emotional and personal feelings, what we call the Last Supper.

Gathered around Jesus were the twelve men who had suffered and shared with Jesus a three-year sojourn unlike anything that will ever again be witnessed in this world. Eleven of them (excepting the apostate traitor Judas Iscariot) had lived a hard three years. To a lesser extent but still noticeably they had lived a rugged life, had been ostracized by some because of their devotion to Christ, and yet for all their human frailties as disciples they were the purest gold. Still, though, they did not fully comprehend the teachings of this Master and were befuddled at some of the shocking things He was saying to them. As yet they really did not know peace and they were most assuredly startled and frightened when Jesus broke the news that He was about to leave them. His eyes scanned the table and doubtless each man there felt that He was talking especially to him only when Christ went to the very soul of their troubles:

> "Let not your heart be troubled; ye believe in God, believe also in me.
>
> In my Father's house are many mansions: if it were not so I would have told you I go to prepare a place for you."

Throughout these few hours' time with them, He often employs that blessed phrase "Fear not" when introducing His thoughts. Then, with that self-awareness that He was the Prince of Peace, again He comforts them with this:

"Peace I leave with you, My peace I give unto you:
not as the world giveth, give I unto you.

Let not your heart be troubled, neither let it be afraid."

The most comforting words indeed from the most comforting man whose footsteps ever tread the earth. Christ surely had demonstrated that with Him peace could be found, and with His presence any problem or situation could be made right. Such a peace is easily understood, and which seeker of peace would not desire His constant presence and companionship. Yet the Prince of Peace has just told them, plainly, undeniably and unmistakably that He was about to leave them. That brief ministry where they had enjoyed His personal care, teaching and friendship was ending, and soon His absence would be marked by a great void. Where now and to whom should they seek the peace, He has promised. Beautifully and exquisitely does Christ provide the answer on both the practical and the theological spheres. Turn to each other, not just they, the apostles, but all Christians for all time and find peace but an infinite number of other treasures as He extols the truest mark of a Christian:

"A new commandment I give unto you, That ye love
one another; as I have loved you that ye also love one
another.

By this shall all men know that ye are my disciples, if
ye have love one to another."

This love and peace, though, expressed so poignantly in beautiful words was to be more than an empty saying, not just a standard which His followers would acknowledge and then ignore. The Son of God, hours only from a scourging which would destroy many men and the Satanic punishment of crucifixion then girded himself with a towel, got on His knees and washed the apostles's feet. This was a task ordinarily performed by the most menial servant, yet here was the Deity Himself in the crisis moment of His earthly life. Here was the true God who came to serve His disciples. The gods of the Greeks and Romans were powerful, often warlike beings, who in their mythologies often killed and conquered, and many of their earthly followers become their disciples with a warrior ethos and a cult of killing and conquering. They were the ones who found peace in destruction, whereas Jesus demonstrated that peace was discovered in brotherly love and service. Truly it is not surprising that in so many ways He, both by word and action, showed that the world's peace and that of God were rooted in deeply different conceptions.

To the disciple, to the Christian, all this is wonderful, yet even Christ's words, examples, admonitions and encouragement do not alter the central fact faced by both the apostles and disciples of all ages. that is the unrelenting truth that the short thirty-three-year life of Jesus was lived in a tiny corner of a century itself two millennia past. We can aid each other, love deeply, serve others unceasingly, but the peach we obtain from one another is still limited, and so was known by Christ Himself. His assurances then revealed a source of peace not fully understood even by the most learned and mature Christian:

> "And I will pray the Father, and He shall give you another Comforter, that He may abide with you forever;

> Even the Spirit of truth; whom the world cannot receive, because it seeth Him not, neither knoweth Him; for He dwelleth with you, and shall be in you."

The solace of these words to the understanding Christian is of a depth which is unfathomable. Christ speaks of that third member of the Trinity, the Being least understood and most misrepresented, and the one over whom Christians still argue with a ferocity that is a shame and disgrace to the name of Christ. The theological questions and disputes concerning the role of the Hole Spirit in the Trinity is certainly not capable of being settled in this short offering, but we are not called upon to do so. The Holy Spirit need only be examined in His role as the Comforter and His continuing effects upon the life of a Christian. Not just with the apostles, but with us as well. Christ reveals to the apostles that the Holy Spirit will be the revelation of the truth, that is the inspiration of the New Testament, written in large part by these apostles. Even more to our examination of peace, though, is the remarkable fact that distinguishes Christians from the world and that is the truth that God Himself in the person of the Holy Spirit lives within us, is our Comforter and directs our steps. In Christ's words there exists the "indwelling" of the spirit that helps the Christian, who guides her in her actions, thoughts and decisions in even the most dire of situations. He is the bringer of peace in the most horrible, the dreariest, the darkest and the most fearful of moments. Because of Him we have the strength to maintain peace at our center, even when plunged into depression, sickness or even death. And how the Comforter does this even the most astute, the most mature, the smartest Christian knows not. It is not important, however, that we know God's methodology in all matters. The Christian can enjoy, even revel in the "...peace that passeth understanding" words that were written many years later by an apostle from a prison cell.

Ultimately, though, we are forced to recognize a dichotomy, an incongruity, in the matter of the presentation of the Prince of Peace to the world, an apparent inconsistency which Christ did little to alleviate and often emphasized. We should and must remember that it was not said of Him but said by Christ Himself that He came not to bring peace, but rather that He was armed with a sword fashioned to divide persons against one another. Yet we can never forget that when He was born the angels themselves heralded "peace on earth" with the coming of this Prince of Peace. Is this a blatant Biblical contradiction which Christians must sadly admit, or may these two concepts still be reconciled? A reconciliation requires an even closer examination of the word "peace" and, ironically, an even closer examination of the word "reconciliation."

It must be admitted, though, it is rarely so stated, that this Prince of Peace, was, is and in this world ever shall remain the most hated man who has ever lived. The common cursory compilation of hated men is usually a short list of such infamous figures as Hitler, Stalin, Mao, Genghis Khan and their ilk. How can anyone possibly assign Christ a higher place on the list of the hated then men such as these, the murderers of tens of millions and the purveyors of nothing but death and destruction? Jesus was described as a man who was so gentle that "...a bruised reed He would not break" and so attentive to all suffering that He was a magnet for children and society's outcasts and dregs and even commented upon the transitory beauty of flowers and the fall of a sparrow. This is the most hated man in history? The few historical names which are sprinkled in this text are long gone. Mass murderers, genocidists and the seeming human incarnations of evil they may be, like us all they were temporal and are now gone. their deviant deeds are history and are buried with them. Jesus Christ, though, must be dealt with, must be confronted, every day in every life lived, just as much today as when He tread the shores of Galilee two thousand years ago. At that most famous of gatherings, the Last Supper, Jesus had much to say to His apostles, the majority of which seemed to bewilder them. As only Christ can do, though, He confronted this issue of conflict and of hatred when He recognized the attitude of the world:

> "If I had not come and spoken unto them, that they had not had sin: but now they have no cloke for their sin."

He spoke this interspersed with His startling revelation to these men that they were to expect hatred at a level and an intensity never seen in this world, but He placed that hatred squarely in context when He revealed:

> "If the world hate you, ye know that it hated me before it hated you."

In this world ever will be it true that Jesus stands supreme as its most hated figure because with Him we can no longer in any manner hide was each of us is, a fallen, floundering sinner who can do nothing to save himself. All this from the Prince of Peace? This is the peace we are told to seek and the man we are directed to emulate? Yes, this is the peace which Christ brings to the inveterate sinner, the apostate, the scoffer and the persecutor, for that person has placed himself at enmity with the Son of God. To these persons Christ brings no peace, and none is intended. No wonder He is hated by them.

The peace which this prince carries is brought to men and women whose natures are every bit as bad as those who reject Him. It is brought to those who are just as fallen, just as condemned but differ in their desire from the worldly. That is the desire to overcome a relationship with God, a connection which was long ago broken and has been restored only by the grace of God and the sacrifice of His Son.

To His only begotten Son the Father had to turn, to the only Being who was sinless, complete and perfect and the only one who could reconcile God with man. Only then can humanity, any man or woman, find peace, which comes through its acceptance and obedience to its author the one who is a prince sitting at the right hand of God Himself, the true Prince of Peace.

THE LION OF JUDAH

Baseball, football, basketball, golf, tennis, an endless array of other sports, entertainment venues, even so recent a cultural phenomenon as rock and roll all have their halls of fame, where their brightest lights and most memorable figures are presumably embedded in memory and honored for time immemorial. The most famous and influential of all books, the Bible, is not lacking a Hall of Fame for its great and memorable historical figures from the Old Testament. In the magnificent New Testament epistle of Hebrews God effectively inventories His "cloud of witnesses," these heroes of the faith, who continually inspire Christians yet today. Many names are called, the most prominent of whom include Noah, Abraham, Sarai, Jacob, Joseph, Moses, David and Samuel, subjects still of study and fascination. The Old Book, though, is a very long tome, and it includes many figures of interest, many exemplary (both good and bad) characters that are not in this "Hall of Fame". Should God in His wisdom have expanded the list, though, or second tier of men and women would have been named persons who while noteworthy do not seem to carry with their historical images the sparkling glitter that the others have. This second tier would likely include a man whose name in a quite unique manner has outlived all the others. This is Judah, the eponymous founder of a people who well into the twenty-first century carry his name, but with opprobrium and with pride – the Jews.

Fortunately, we are not lacking information regarding this man, the fourth of twelve sons of the great Hebrew patriarch, Jacob, and the older brother of a man more greatly revered, Joseph. Unlike his younger sibling Joseph, whose entire life seems to have been a path of earthly fame and spiritual splendor, Judah does not have an auspicious beginning. The story of Joseph's betrayal by his brothers, one of the foundational narratives of history and the scriptures, needs not another retelling here. Yet we are to be reminded that Joseph's older brothers originally sought not just betrayal, but they wished to murder their upstart seventeen-year-old brother, the "golden" child of father Jacob. It was Judah's intervention, though, which spared his life when Judah objected to outright murder. Why not sell him into slavery to the passing Ishmaelites and make a little money for ourselves he suggested. So, they did, and Judah became a betrayer and a slave dealer, but at least his hands were clean of murder.

As the years passed Judah became a man of some wealth and substance, with an extended family of many heirs. Judah, though, apparently possessed an abundance of faults common to many men. In an involved story recorded in Genesis Judah is unsurprisingly shown as a man who does not always honor his promises and also as a man given to the most basic human temptations, illicit sexual lust, and lust overtly acted upon. He engaged the services of a young woman that he mistook for a prostitute and likely let the incident quickly recede in his memory. Three months later his widowed daughter-in-law is found to be pregnant. With his patriarchal authority and grandeur

Judah condemns her to death, yet Tamar has a surprise for Judah, proof that she and his presumed prostitute are one and the same person. Mortified and ashamed, Judah has her freed, and he recognizes his own greater guilt. Judah's overall conduct had been appalling, yet his courage in admitting his sin and confessing his guilt goes not unnoticed.

Judah's greatest and most important role on the Biblical stage had yet to be played. At least thirteen years elapsed, and the fortunes of Joseph and his brothers have reversed. Fulfilling the long-term Divine plans Joseph's status went from lowly Egyptian prisoner to the brilliant and successful prime minister of Egypt, second only to Pharaoh himself, all the while maintaining a sterling moral character. Judah and his brothers had come to Egypt for desperately needed relief from a seven-year famine, and Joseph recognized them. Through a series of intrigues orchestrated by Joseph himself, this younger scorned brother now held his own would-be murderers in the palm of his hand. Joseph decreed that all the brothers save one, the youngest Benjamin, the now personal favorite of father Jacob could return to their homes. Benjamin, though, would remain in Egypt as this great prime minister's personal slave. The eleven brothers, three of them older than Judah, are transfixed in fear before the mighty one, as yet unknown to them as their younger brother, Joseph. Judah, though, demonstrates that it is he who has become the real leader of the family, as he steps forward and pleads with Joseph that he, Judah, be taken as the sacrificial slave, so that his brothers might live. Joseph is moved to tears by this act of courage, and in a scene of dramatic magnificence reveals to his brothers that he is their brother, Joseph. The inescapable interpretation is that Joseph was so moved by Judah's act of courage in saving his brother Benjamin, in saving his father Jacob from fatal grief and in saving God's plans for humanity's redemption.

The great book of Genesis concludes with the story of the patriarch Jacob's transmittal of the family blessing to the chosen son, and this was a matter of immense importance in these ancient, patriarchal days. It was not given to Joseph, the most splendid of his sons, but still the next to youngest in a brood of twelve. To each of his sons Jacob presented special words of description, but it was to Judah that the most special and foretelling were given. Jacob related that:

> "Judah, thou art he whom thy brethren shall praise;
> thy hand shall be in the neck of thine enemies; thy
> father's children shall bow down before thee.
>
> Judah is a lion's whelp..."

It was through this fourth son that the great promise originally given to Abraham would be manifested and fulfilled. Through Judah, this lion, would come one far greater than he, and as for Judah his symbol forever would be that of a lion, which literally became the recognized emblem of the tribe of Judah.

But why a lion? What is/was a lion, and why would be given such a prominent role in the theology of God? The people of the Old Testament world were certainly acquainted with lions, but it was of a slightly different sort than we know today. These Bible lands were regions in which roamed the Asiatic, or Persian lion, somewhat smaller than the breed with which out twenty-first century eyes gaze, the African lion. The Persian lion was a bit smaller, at most three feet at the shoulders and five feet long, yet it was in character and personality every bit the lion we know today. Like all members of the cat family, from the loveable domestic cat to the magnificently grand Bengal tiger the lion is inherently graceful. Like all cats, the most graceful and elegant of four-footed creatures it treads the earth with a serenity and quietness unmatched by any other creature. The lion's tawny coat is the covering of an animal possessing surprisingly great power. Coupled with its speed and quickness the lion's power makes it one of the world's most feared predators. Its power and strength is all the more surprising for the lion, like most cats, is basically meek, knowing how to conserve energy and strength and expending such only when necessary. Stated otherwise a lion is so expert at being a lion that he does not need to continually display that strength, but all the wise know that it abides.

All cats, from new-born kittens to the mighty lions, tigers, cheetahs and leopards possess an inborn inherent dignity. Yes, any cat, even a lion, may be abused, maltreated, hurt or tortured, but it retains a God-given dignity that never absents itself. Throw a cat in water, which they hate, and he emerges with a look not of humiliation, but with a feeling of contempt for his abuser. Slay him, if you will, and even the memory of his dignity will mock you. Lions are truly among God's noblest creatures.

We may sing indefinite hymns of praise to the lion, but he is perhaps most noted and admired for two qualities. So strong and noble is the lion that he is forever known as the "King of Beasts." Many organizations and nations, most notably Great Britain have long sported a lion as a national emblem of strength and courage. Almost one thousand years ago one of England's most celebrated monarchs, Richard II, became known and is still acclaimed as Richard the Lionhearted, for his battlefield prowess. Yet we do not need to examine King Richard of old any further, but we should take notice of that compound worded title "Lionhearted" implying both the man's bravery and that other quality for which the lion is famous, courage. We are reminded that Judah was called by his father Jacob, a lion's cub, and Jacob's fourth son increasingly grew in moral stature and courage to merit the name.

71

Thankfully, lions remain with us as fellow residents of the world, but naturally Judah, the Old Testament hero, is, of course, long removed from this earth. Let us not, though, be led astray by a point which we could easily confuse. While Judah developed the leonine attributes of dignity and courage, Judah himself was in no sense the Lion of Judah. He was the ancestor to the true Lion of Judah revealed to us in the Bible's final book:

"Behold the Lion of the tribe of Judah, the Root of David."

This is no prophecy for such is no longer required, the true Lion of Judah having come in the person of Jesus Christ. How strange it seems that the Prince of Peace is one and the same person as the Lion of Judah. At first reading one's initial reaction is that one of these names is a misnomer, for how could one be both a purveyor of peace and a predator? This demands a closer examination not only of the character but also of the history of Jesus Christ viewed in conjunction with that very title, the Lion of Judah.

The baby borne in that manger in Bethlehem so long ago had an earthly pedigree that in so many ways has never been matched. The Gospel writers Mathew and Luke painstakingly enumerate His ancestry all the way to the beginning, the "genesis" so to speak, and name generation by generation each of His progenitors, among them Judah, followed by a man named Perez. Who was Perez, one may logically inquire? We are now to remember the liaison between Judah and the presumed prostitute, actually his daughter-in-law, Tamar. The issue of that tryst was Perez, as with them all an indispensable link in the generational history of Jesus. Firmly implanted in the Tribe of Judah, Christ's ancestors most famously included King David, who fourteen

generations prior to the Messiah firmly established a royal and courageous reputation.

But again, our Savior's predator, a killer? Do we celebrate the
beauty of His life and character by adding those two traits to His per-
sona? In no way, for it is the other traits of character, magnificently
presented and defined in the animal kingdom by the lion but taken to
their Divine apogee by Christ that we honor.

Foremost of those character traits which we honor in the Lion
of Judah is one that is not prominent in the teachings of Christ, and
that is His courage, displayed in all forms and with all persons, both
friend and foe. Except for King Herod the Great, from his nationality
to age thirty Jesus of Nazareth attracted little or no notice from the
high and the mighty. Actually, if Jesus was simply a "good" man or
a "good" teacher that so many people have traditionally declaimed
Him He likely would have continued to attract a minimum of attention and would have caused very little fear or apprehension from civil
or religious authority. Maybe He would have been to many, in that
particularly semi-sophisticated warped thinking of the world, just a
quaint, harmless teacher, of which the Jews were known to produce a
plethora of examples. To limit Christ to such a role, though, is remarkably blinkered and short-sighted. He had the courage to go against the
established religious authorities and doctrine of the day, not because
they were established, not because they were in authority, and not because they were teachings. He stood and spoke against them because
they were wrong.

Christ recognized that what burdened the people was not just the
small coteries of priests, religious scholars and zealots but rather the
general miasma of popular religious opinion, which so many, then
and now, take as absolute truth. When we read and study the most
famous address ever given, the Sermon on the Mount, it is stunning

the frequency with which Jesus introduces each topic with the phrase "Ye have heard..." In each instance He proceeds to show that what we "hear" and the actual truth about matters are often strangers one to another. One by one Christ revealed that what the multitude had come to believe (usually prompted by the religious authorities) was wrong on important subjects such as uncontrolled anger, adultery, sexual morality, vengeance, hatred, love and forgiveness was plainly wrong. It is relatively easy to point out wrong, but so much more difficult to point out the right. Christ had the knowledge and the courage to do both. When we read His teachings and contemplate and comprehend the oppositional settings in which He often delivered then we worship Him for His courage and just as were His original audience, we are "astonished" at the authority with which He taught.

Not alone with words did Christ display the courage of a lion, and the four gospels are replete with stories in which the bravery of His conduct was as astonishing as were His words. He had the courage to mingle and associate with anyone, and we repeat for emphasis, anyone. First century Judea was obviously markedly different than any twenty-first century modern nation, but the differences were equaled by certain uniformities of thought and behavior. As in all societies, certain persons and classes were elevated above the norm, while others were degraded in the eyes of society. Two groups who not only were on a low rung on the societal ladder, but arguably had dropped off the ladder entirely were the publicans and "sinners" which often in their terminology was a term employed interchangeably with prostitute. Publicans were the tax collectors for the forcibly imposed Roman state, were looked upon as traitors and with great accuracy often viewed as morally corrupt individuals. The scribes and Pharisees pounced upon an opportunity to condemn Jesus and murmured against Him.

"Why do ye eat and drink with publicans and sinners?"

He patiently replied that His association was not His stamp of approval but rather a means to call them away from their sins. Human nature, then and now, even among Christians is to associate primarily with what modern sociology has deemed our own socio-economic group. In other words, we wish to be with people who are like us. Jesus, though, possessed a courage to step away from this and give time and attention to anyone who needed Him, for as He said, "I came not to call the righteous, but sinners to repentance." He thus came for everybody.

It takes real courage to break down social barriers. Certainly, the ancients were not immune to false or pretended courage, but in out modern times we are neck deep in phony bravado. Real courage is not displayed in writing newspaper and magazine articles to a readership that is likely to agree with the author. Real courage is not displayed by internet users, who range from what are derogatorily called trolls to self-presumed sophisticated bloggers writing daring and even threatening messages from the comforts of their homes and lairs, often draped in a cloak of anonymity. Authentic bravery is not found in a politician, no matter their presumed eloquence (which, in an aside, is almost non-existent today) strutting and prancing and crooning words of moral courage to an audience often raucously partisan and imbued with venom towards any opposition, real or presumed.

The authentic, genuine article, the real courage is most often found in action, and an action which produces or at least tries to produce constructive desires. This is the courage which the Lion of Judah, Jesus Christ, had in super abundance.

One day on an early mission of His ministry Jesus and His apostles, all Jews and proud Jews, traveling to His home in Galilee, made a brief rest stop in Samaria. The animosity and hatred of the Samaritans and Jews is still so well known that it needs not another retelling, other than to state that it had long historical antecedents and was racially biased. While Christ was sitting by a well, a Samaritan woman came to draw her daily requirements of water. Boldly, even shockingly, Christ exploded social barriers with a mere four simple words spoken to the Samaritan woman:

"Give me to drink."

Ordinarily, as we have stated, the Samaritans and Jews had no dealings with one another. Some Jews so adamant in their disgust and hatred for the Samaritans that they would re-route a journey, so they did not even pass through Samaria. The lady herself synopsized well the Jewish-Samaritan relationship when she replied:

"How is it that thou, being a Jew, askest drink of me, which am a woman of Samaria? for the Jews have no dealings with the Samaritans."

Yet the conversation continued, and the barrier of ethnic prejudice toppled, not by a speech nor by legislation or decree but by human action, courageous human action.

The meeting with Jesus and this woman was remarkable for the noted factors alone, but perhaps an even greater obstacle was overcome by the courage of Christ. This was a time and, in a society, where men and women held such rigidly defined roles that it was a major social faux pas for a woman to publicly speak to a man who was neither her husband nor relative. This was not scripture or the Law of Moses, but rather human tradition, a tradition that impeded the spread of the Truth. Christ had no hesitation in stepping outside the cultural constraints and talking to a woman. Neither did the woman, a remarkable person herself who openly and freely spoke with this man who she perceived to be a prophet. The scriptures fully develop this narrative of Christ's encounter and conversation with the Samaritan woman, and it is a deep reservoir of moral instruction. It also provides one of the best examples of a remarkable phenomenon, and that is the relationship which Christ had with women. The state of women at the time of Christ's coming has already been the subject of brief remarks. Those long centuries which preceded His Coming are little different, and yet today, in a drastically changed world, the relationship between the sexes remains the subject of many questions. With Jesus Christ it was different. Consistently, many times over, women of all ages, different ethnic backgrounds, likely of radically different physical appearances approached this Master from Galilee, and approached Him in the seeming certainty that here was a man who would treat them honorably and with respect, not looking upon her with ravenous personal emotions, but truly as a sister to a loving brother. Neither before nor after has any man, even those with the best hearts and intentions, established the rapport with women that Christ found.

We are judged by our associates and friends. Particularly when a person is younger, he/she wishes to be noted as the member of a "cool" group, one with certain characteristics, some of which are tangible and some more ethereal. Depending on age, culture and other social factors the average individual would aspire to friendship and association with the wealthy, the better educated, those from cities of note and fame. In His life Christ had the courage not to flaunt these prevailing conditions but rather simply to ignore them. Nowhere is this revealed more than His selection of the twelve men to be the apostles, the very foundation of the Church. Perhaps the most important group of selected men in history, they came not from the high priesthood, were not noted religious scholars and had little social standing. The majority were Galilean fishermen, blue collar men with backwater ways and accents with the one notable exception, the apostle Matthew, being of all things...a publican, even worse. This selection displayed Divine Wisdom, and it also demonstrated a profound courage.

While the life of Jesus Christ remains a symposium on courage it is His Passion, His Death, where the bravery of the Son of Man attains a pinnacle which has never and will never be reached. His willing sacrifice through the agony and excruciating pain of His crucifixion is the central point of His life, His earthly mission, but it is something even more. These events are the centerpiece of human existence, the reason every human life was created and the existential reason for being. They provide meaning to every baby's birth, to every person's life, and truly to every breath that is drawn. Without them life is truly meaningless, nihilistic abyss, a void of horror too terrible to contemplate. With Christ and His sacrifice, though, everything becomes infused with meaning and each moment of life, a gift itself, is a portent of a perfect eternity to come. All this glory, this wonder, the promise of the "abundant life" and the enticement of Heaven, did not have to be. It all comes from the sacrifice of God, the willingness of His Son to be sacrificed and the courage, unfaltering courage, of Jesus. We each have a choice to accept the life which the Son of God offered, but how little attention is given to the fact that Christ Himself had a choice. He did not have to make this sacrifice.

All flesh, every man and woman, partakes of suffering in this life, but rarely is it done willingly. Christ, this Man of Sorrows, was no conscript to pain and suffering, for He volunteered for the cross. As He told His apostles:

> "I lay down my life... No man taketh it from me, but
> I lay it down of Myself. I have power to lay it down,
> and I have power to take it again."

How pathetic are the old arguments over who killed Christ, the Jews, the Romans, the Pharisees, ad infinitum? If the soldiers had not placed His body on the cross, He would have placed it there Himself. Every drop of blood shed, every lash of the scourging whip, every insult, every catcall and taunt, He suffered not of necessity but because of His voluntary desire and love to redeem mankind. This Lion of Judah demonstrated courage beyond our understanding the courage of the disciple's Lion of Judah unfailingly inspires us, but it is an inspiration shadowed by darkness. The lion of Judah is not alone, for the world is a hunting ground for another lion, this one a predator, the greatest predator of all, Satan. Our Lion of Judah is also the Lamb of God, but this lion is described as:

"...your adversary, the devil, as a roaring lion, walketh about, seeking whom he may devour."

He is a savage beast and the due to this Devil is that he has always succeeded in capturing the majority of souls. The days of his Satanic majesty, though, dwindle in numbers, and he, too, will be a witness to the eternal triumph of the true Lion of Judah.

{ 6 }

THE GREAT PHYSICIAN

In 1811 England William Hunter was born and as a small child he emigrated with his parents to the burgeoning land of America, and settled in the town of York, Pennsylvania. Later he became a respected Methodist minister and authored a poem of seven stanzas, the first and most famous of which is:

> "The Great Physician now is near, the sympathizing
> Jesus;
> He speaks the drooping heart to cheer, oh, hear the
> name of Jesus."

Not long thereafter another Methodist minister, John Hart Stockton, set these words to music, and the frequent usage of this hymn ever since has given it , "The Great Physician" a high place in the Christian musical canon. The simplicity and tenderness of its lyrics coupled with the lilting, yet haunting, uplift of its melody, have given succor to endless numbers of the fearful and suffering. The music has also done much to implant in the Christian community an irresistible image of the humble Jesus of Nazareth as the Great Physician. That title, among the dozens upon dozens given Him in the scriptures is surely one of a half-dozen most widely used. Stunningly, though, nowhere does the New Testament itself refer to Jesus as the "Great Physician" is as many words, yet before we dismiss the title as being an artificial creation of its author, let us consider that Christ referenced Himself as a physician when He exclaimed that "They that be whole need not a physician." He also knew that it was a term of derision which was flung in His face with the epithet "Physician, heal thyself." So, to all He was a physician, and if any man ever deserved the title it was Christ. Too, no disciple would deny that He was great, so Jesus wears well the mantel of The Great Physician.

Christ's personal practice as a "physician" was conducted in the setting of a very small space and time, first century Judea for a span of but a few years. It would be pedantic in the extreme to make a detailed case about how physicians and medical practice differ in the first and twenty-first centuries. Even the finest physicians practiced under severe strictures, primarily lack of any sophisticated knowledge about either the human body or the cause and nature of the diseases which would ravage it. Any drugs and medications were very limited, and doubtless the ideas of homeopathy and naturalism were found in their extreme forms. The physicians themselves, although most were likely intelligent and well meaning knew less about the human body than a reasonably educated person today.

We may state with certainty that in the main, physicians drew their patients from the same source as they do today, that is those persons who desire the alleviation of pain, to feel better or if necessary, to be fully cured or healed. No doubt most ancient physicians tried with all their efforts but except for those ailments or injuries which can today be healed by a non-physician at a walk-in clinic the efficacy of their professional services was extremely limited.

The initial impulse is to assert that as a physician Jesus was a general practitioner, but a closer examination indicates the inaccuracy of such a statement. As a physician, though, Christ was far removed from a general practice. A generalist offers a variety of cures, medications and prescriptions, and being fully desirous to have as many patients as possible his door and practice are open to all. Christ, however, was and is different. The Great Physician knew from the beginning that overwhelmingly His services had no interest to the masses of mankind, and we are reminded of His statement that "They that be whole need not a physician." Roughly translated it would appear that Christ is stating that should a person feel no need for His services, then He had none to offer. Likely it was His own mother Mary who touched upon this when in her Magnificat she exclaimed that "…the rich He has sent away empty." This was no particular blow or slander to the wealthy but rather an intimation that this physician has nothing to offer the whole, the self-satisfied or the proud. But who is or ever has been whole in and of himself? All who have ever drawn a breath in this earth at one point or another have need of a physician, and most have the self-awareness to admit such. The spiritual remedies of the Great Physician comprise an enormous cache of medication that the majority never draw upon or even contemplate such. His services remain unknown and untouched by the masses of humanity.

Turn we now, though, to those who come to avail themselves of what He has to offer. since He is called a physician, who are His patients and what are their needs? Initially, Christ has it better than most physicians since He is spared one of the banes of the practice of medicine, the hypochondriac. Dictionaries provide an increasing list of definitions for this word, but suffice it to say that its common understanding is the person whose illness is imagined, or at a minimum, grossly exaggerated. No spiritual hypochondriac ever made an appointment to see the Great Physician, for there exist no men or women with "imagined" spiritual needs. Jesus stated that He called all men everywhere to repentance, and He is the one doctor who never turns away patients.

One of the saddest, the most tragic of existential truths is that those who need the Great Physician the most are those that heed Him the least. Billions upon billions of sick souls have passed a brief sojourn on this earth with but little or no thought of the Great Physician. They have lived lives within the normal range of human experience, happiness, brief contentment, brief moments of joy, but even more of heartache, drudgery, toil and misery and unanswered questions of "What's it all for?" All have carried their share of sins, untreated by any practitioner, sins in many cases so great, long lasting and mortifying that their very souls seemingly begin to putrefy. All is lived and done and as yet proceeds absent the services of the one true healing hand, that of the Great Physician. Employing the current parlance, the multitudes are "in denial" about their desperate condition, and Christ can do nothing for them.

We return now for an examination and analysis of those that do come to Christ and the reasons for their actions. Almost all humanity (perhaps it would be better to drop the word "almost") suffer pain. Yes, physical pain is part of the fabric of life, but here, though, we speak of the mental, emotional and spiritual suffering which all endure. The Great Physician was never slack in the number and the grandeur of the claims which He made of His skills regarding the alleviation of pain and distress. Yet more than this, in His brief earthly ministry He showcased and demonstrated His ability at pain alleviation and at curing longstanding problems, and His demonstrations revealed the competency and completeness of His healing methodology.

Early in His teachings Jesus went to a pool in Jerusalem. Its name was Bethesda, and it was a mineral spring, the waters of which periodically stirred, and were thought to provide if not outright healing, at least restorative relief for those handicapped and disabled persons fortunate enough to get in the pool at the appropriate time. One who continually visited the pool but who was not among the fortunate was a man who had been deformed and crippled for thirty-eight years. Others always got ahead of him in the scramble to get to the water, and for almost four decades he suffered until... Christ saw him and in response to the man's desire to be cured Christ merely and plainly said:

"Rise, take up they bed and walk."

Miraculously, he did just that and the Great Physician's words to him expressed the nature of His cure:

"...thou art made whole."

Not a little better, not just the promise of something better in a vaguely defined future but "whole" and with an immediacy which was stunning. No serious Christian maintains and posits that such immediate, miraculous all-encompassing healings occur today. Neither Jesus of Nazareth nor any of His apostles now tread the earth. The reality of the healing of the long-time crippled man and countless others of the lane, the halt and the blind still serve in magnificent glory as emblems of the spiritual and the emotional healing which only Christ can offer.

Certain elements and traits have a universality among humanity, and suffering is certainly in the upper reaches of the list. Unless a person is totally self-deluded men and women recognize at least in part that some of their suffering is occasioned by their own actions, at times their own self-willed conduct. Regardless, though, it is still suffering, and emotional pain and spiritual depths are still found. Christ, not only the Great Physician but the Universal Physician does not turn such patients away. The modern era of specialized highly technological medical treatment has been midwife to many specialized medical facilities, hospitals, clinics and treatment centers, such as those limited to neurological, heart or cancer problems. It is truly a benefit to live in such a time where the skills of already highly skilled professionals are concentrated and focused on a few or perhaps even only one type of illness. Undoubtedly, most are legitimate, but it has been alleged that certain medical centers and professionals infiltrate their "cure" percentage by accepting those they deem most easy to cure. The Great Physician is the diametrical opposite of such, as He takes those patients whose illness and suffering is of long tenure and deeply rooted.

Not just physical illness. Early one morning Jesus was teaching in the temple when suddenly the scribes and Pharisees burst in unannounced, escorting a young woman against her will, an episode that will claim the attention of any audience, anywhere, at any time. With the smugness and self-righteous pride of a hunter who has bagged his prey and is now expecting to lay claim to even bigger game they defiantly challenge Christ and His teaching:

> "They say unto Him, Master, this woman was taken
> in adultery, in the very act.

Now Moses in the law commanded us, that such
should be stoned: but what sayest thou."

So, they now had their prey cornered. Should Jesus ignore or
even downplay the adultery that would be a blatant violation of the
Mosarcial Law and undermine any religious authority He might
claim. Should He rule her worthy of death He would run afoul of the
Romans, who had taken from the Jews the authority to impose capital punishment. So, what was this new teacher of supposedly strange
doctrines to do. Neither for the first and certainly not for the last time,
Jesus did the unexpected. He began writing in the dirt and all the
would-be prosecutors left the woman alone with Christ. This side of
eternity no one will ever know the words which He inscribed in this
tablet of dirt, but we are now informed of the ensuing conversation
between Christ and the woman. Christ arose from the ground and gently asked her:

"Woman, where are thine accusers? hath no man condemned thee?'

Upon her response that she was now without their condemnation
He further added:

"Neither do I condemn thee: go, and sin no more."

So much of the glorious character of Jesus Christ is revealed in
this one incident. His calmness and refusal to accept the bait which
the Pharisees had thrown Him was the beginning of the unraveling of
their plans. His quiet, even silent, response in simply writing something in the dirt always captures the audience's attention. Many spec-
ulations have been offered regarding what He wrote, among them that

perhaps in some way He catalogued the sins of those who accused her. Whatever the wording it was surely effective, but it lacked the high drama of the only words which He directed at the accusers:

"He that is without sin among you, let him first cast
a stone at her."

The lessons offered by Christ's conduct and His very few words in this narrative are layered and deep. It is rightly seen as a condemnation of finger-pointing and judgmental conduct when the accuser's sins may be as great as those of the accused. Self-absorption and self-righteousness are condemned in the New Testament and condemned without exception. It, too, is an illustration of mercy, for Jesus had earlier proclaimed "Blessed are the merciful." In their ravenous haste to trap Christ the Pharisees basically treated this humiliated woman as an inanimate object. As an aside, it should be noted that while they captured the woman in the "very act" of adultery, somehow the adulterous man escaped their clutches. Their lack of mercy is in sharp contrast to that shown by Christ to these same accusatory Pharisees. One by one He easily could have inventoried their sins to all within earshot, but instead He gave them an avenue of retreat.

For our present purposes, though, perhaps the greatest moral lesson from this incident is shown in how the Great Physician practices His profession. Whatever her sins, and likely they had been great, Christ knew that she needed comfort as well as a healing cure. For comfort He gave her defense against a mob bent on the destruction of both she and the Savior and the physician's prescription that went to the heart of her problem:

"Go, and sin no more."

To note a final irony the Pharisees did one thing right. They brought her to Christ.

As a physician Jesus had many specialties, one of which remains exclusive to Himself and the exclusivity abides to this day. He is the Great Physician to the incurable and the hopeless. It is a natural and normal human trait to avoid the hopeless and any situation that contains no promise of betterment. It is not natural for us to admit another fact, equally as true as the previous, and that is the salient reality that we are reluctant to be around hopeless persons. Very few wish to spend their hours in the company of those in the last stages of terminal illness, the severely retarded, those in a coma and maybe most of all the grotesquely insane. "Insane" is a word not in as much common circulation as it was previously, but unfortunately it is still descriptive of many. Christ is the one physician who never recoiled from the mentally, physically and especially the spiritually "hopeless" and in fact the skills of the Great Physician are here displayed in the brightest light.

Adjacent to Christ's homeland of Galilee was Gadara, and there lived a man who to many had doubtless sunk below any level of recognized common humanity:

> "...(T)here met Him out of the city a certain man,
> which had devils long time, and wore no clothes, nei-
> ther abode in any house but in the tombs."

Whether we admit it or deny it, even the best of men and women reflexively avoid such a person, whether the homeless, a panhandler on the street and most certainly very few visit modern institutions in which they live. Not so with Christ. Tormented incessantly by devils the man's life may have provided a preview of an existence in hell. His customary state was duly and hideously described:

"...Oftentimes the (unclean spirit) caught him: and
he was kept bound with chains and in fetters; and he
break the banks, and was driving of the devil into the
wilderness."

By anyone's standards physically, emotionally and spiritually this
man had already edged into the nether regions, and was in as desperate condition as may be found by any creature in this world. Repellant,
repugnant and foul yet Christ approached him and cast the offending
demons from him. The devils then were compelled by Christ into a
feeding herd of swine (an illegal, unclean animal) and they all perished when the maddened pigs ran violently over a cliff to be drowned
in a lake. The insane man's recovery was amazing, quickly done and
fully complete. When a modern patient visits even the best physician
that patient, if reasonable, does not automatically expect either an immediate or even a full cure. The Great Physician provided both, and
we now see the tortured man in a different light:

"(They) found the man, out of whom the devils were
departed, sitting at the feet of Jesus, clothed, and in
his right mind."

The list of Christ's publicly unpopular patients is a long one.
While Christ was passing through Jericho one day a little man named
Zacchaeus scrambled to see the passing Master. The normal crowd
obscured his view, so he climbed a sycamore tree, the better to see
the Savior. Many always came to see Christ, but this Zacchaeus held
a special distinction. He was no "natural" disciple inasmuch as he was
one of the hated Roman-employed tax collectors, a publican. Yet, not
only was he a publican but also the scriptures pointedly designate him
as the chief publican and thereby a very rich man. As He passed Jesus

hailed Zacchaeus and bid him descend from the sycamore, as Christ invited Himself to stay at the home of this strange little man. Amidst a disapproving background murmur of the multitude Zacchaeus came down and went with Christ to his home.

So, moved by the attention which Christ paid to him and the recipient of one of the most famous doctor's house calls in history Zacchaeus stood and proclaimed:

> "Lord, the half of my goods I give to the poor; and if
> I have taken anything from any man by false accusa-
> tion, I restore him fourfold."

An elated Christ, the attending, the curing physician then pronounced the results of treatment, an announcement that should be among the most coveted words any person would wish to hear:

> "This day is salvation come to this house."

This was the spiritual equivalent taken to an infinite power of a doctor, telling the patient and those that love him that the terminal cancer and the dread of imminent death has been removed. The Great Physician's cure, given to a willing patient, enjoys a success rate of one hundred percent.

The question is rightfully posed, though, is how effective is the Great Physician and His methods with the unwilling and the unaccepting? Untold numbers of patients visit doctors on a daily basis, with all sorts of treatments, plans and medicines continually prescribed, yet some estimates are that in America along almost two-thirds of prescriptions for drugs and medicines are never even filled. We may wonder, even without benefit of statistical survey, at how many recommendations for exercise programs and dietary plans are basically ignored. In plain words, many, perhaps even a majority of patients, reject the advice of their physicians, no matter how sound and cogent that advice may be. The reasons for such rejection are beyond the scope of this essay, but a few offer themselves as plain suggestion. Lack of self-awareness as to the reality of one's true condition or perhaps self-satisfaction of the current state must be prime reasons. Patients are infected with the same traits as is all the population, that is a basic conservative unwillingness to change and a deadening inertia of being. Underlying all, though, may be an inherent belief that it is better not to change, for my "certain" present is likely better than an uncertain and unsettled future. More than any doctor who ever lived it is likely that Christ had a greater number of this sort of patient than any physician who ever lived.

A quite unusual and in so many respects admirable young man came to Christ – not only did he just come to Jesus but the scriptures state that "…there came one running, and kneeled to Him." Eagerness, respect and obeisance were all shown to Christ, and the scriptures remarked that Jesus "beholding him love him." He had a question for Christ, the answer to which he likely presumed would reinforce his life and direct his bright future. "What shall I do to inherit eternal life." he asked, a question, if not on the lips of at least in the heart of every rational sentient being. Keep the commandments directed Christ, those basic moral precepts which direct any decent life. Abstain from murder, adultery, theft, lying and so forth, which must have been ecstatic news to the young man, as he responded that he had kept these from his youth and "…what lack I yet?" This good man, but likely with the flaw of too much self-assurance received a devastating blow when Christ told him:

> "One thing thou lackest: go thy way, sell whatsoever thou hast, and give to the poor and thou shalt have treasures in heaven."

The Great Physician's prescription was too strong for the young man and he "...went away grieved, for he had great possessions." Only Christ can give the answer to this, but it may be unlikely that he wished the man to abandon everything. He did, however, demonstrate that for a variety of reasons his means of justification were in error. Among those items he surely coveted were: (1) the approval of Christ for the life he had already lived, and (2) in those words which Christ used elsewhere a recognition that he truly was "whole" and needed no physician. Even performing the works which Christ outlined for Him would not have saved him. He rejected the same prescription for salvation that so many turn aside, and that is that salvation comes from acceptance of Christ as the Savior and the obedience to His Word. None of us is whole of ourselves, and all need the services of the Great Physician.

The multitudes always have and sadly always will reject the services of the Great Physician. The majority's rejection is found in simply ignoring Him, but a small minority actively oppose. Sadly, for Him but more for them an even smaller minority actively mock Him. While on Calvary's Cross:

> "...the people...and the rulers...derided Him, saying, He saved others; let Him save Himself, if He be Christ the chosen of God."

> "...and the soldiers also mocked Him..."

The Great Physician's response, though, remained one of healing:

"Father, forgive them; for they know not what they do."

{ 7 }

ALPHA AND OMEGA

Who makes the rules? This is literally a timeless eternal question which predates the existence of mankind. To the Christian believer it is a question which predates our own world, which is itself an arena for the great contest of competing authorities. Only briefly referenced in the scriptures is a rebellion in Heaven itself. A rebellion occurring before the earthly measurement of time, an insurrection in which Satan attempted to supplant God Himself as the ruler of the universe. He suffered defeat and that defeat, and his subsequent actions still provide a major force and factor in all humanity's existence. Yet the opening pages of the Bible still reflect that the contest for authority had no cessation with Satan's fall from Heaven.

The demand for authority, such a desired treasure by many is a fire that has burned and raged from the earth's beginning and shows no signs at all of any abatement. As Christ Himself once remarked there shall always exist "wars and rumors of wars" and no deep historical knowledge is required to understand that almost all wars are at base a contest and a drive that some men possess to assert their power and authority over other men. Whether their impetus and/or their rationale be the conquest of nations, races, religions or just the personal power aggrandizement of the progenitor's wars are fought for domination, so that one person or a group of people can assert and exercise their will and power over others.

We should be hesitant, though, to limit the desire for authority to something as grandiose and dramatic as war. The desire for office and position is likely fathered by many desires and emotions but central to most is that desire to "make the rules." In a representative government legislators are referenced as law "makers," judges issue "rulings" and "decrees" and executives and administrators dispense "orders." Yet we would be short-sighted to limit this drive for authority to our political classes. Whatever may be their psyche many persons see any human relationship as the opportunity to exert power, to coerce and force their will upon others. Vast numbers of individuals have proven inept and even incapable of exercising authority in the most private relationships. In the workplace a person may have under authority one or more employees and all are present to perform designated tasks and goals, yet the manager or supervisor views it essentially as a means to exert power. Even more importantly is the domestic situation, bliss to the fortunate and on the far side of a purgatory to others. Nothing screams abuse more than a marital situation in which the two parties see it as a forum for the exercise of authority. Usually men, they view it as just one more opportunity to press forward their own private agenda and make others bend to their will. It is on the whole a sickenly distorted and perverted view of actual authority.

So, authority has, is and always will be abused, and the abuse will be on stages both vast and petty. Authority remains an essential, though, for on this earth, inhabited by fallen human beings, very little can be accomplished in its absence. In fact, without its substance and structure everything descends into anarchy and chaos. Does anybody actually have true authority? This question is answered with a resounding yes, but with this answer comes a realization that true authority is a valuable, precious and exclusive commodity, given to one man only, as Christ announced:

"All power is given unto me in heaven and in earth."

With that striking brevity of words, He always employed Jesus established the exclusivity and the limits of His authority. He alone possesses the real article, and He is subject to no limitations. Throughout its pages the Bible treats authority as a matter of the highest importance, its correct assertion praised, and its frequent abuse condemned. The reading of the subject demands closer attention, and at least two and easily more questions immediately arise. First, if Jesus of Nazareth is the sole owner of this authority, we wish to know how He employs it. It follows then that if He was given all He was also given the right to assign its usage to others of His choosing and for His purposes.

Christ's authority and its exercise are not self-generated, and always He made clear that whatever He had was given Him by His own Father. The times and occasions in which He interjected that all He had came from His Father in Heaven are too abundant and numerous to cite. Likely His greatest explanation of the origin of authority is from a confrontation which Christ had with a very powerful and self-important man, someone who no one would characterize as a man of God. In the first century province of Judea the Roman governor was not merely an important man but rather he was the important man, answerable only to the emperor in Rome. He literally held life and death power over those he ruled, and it was this very power of which Pontius Pilate was keenly and boastfully aware early on a Friday morning a long time ago. Already beaten half to death by a Roman scourging the bloodied Jesus stood before Pilate, who began to pepper Him with questions, His reply to all being silence. Finally, an exasperated Governor Pilate with the full might of Rome at his back swaggeringly threatened Jesus, a man whom the governor knew to be innocent with his hissing words of menace:

> "Speakest thou not unto me? Knowest thou not that I
> have power to crucify thee, and have power to release
> thee?"

Christ, beaten, whipped, likely sickened by pain finally opens His curtain of silence:

> "Thou couldst have no power at all against me, except
> it were given thee from above..."

The body of Jesus had been severely beaten, but the truth and impact of these words may have drained the color from Pilate's face and caused his knees to weaken. No man who appeared before him had ever spoken such words, for this prisoner had stripped Pilate bare of his pretensions to power. You have no power on your own account and none from Rome's account either, he had been told. All your power is given you from the source of all authority, God. In other words, Pilate, you may have soldiers at your back, yet they are not holding back the angry, stirring, tumultuous Jewish mob. Pilate, your power is at the pleasure of my Father, and it may be removed from you in the blink of an eye. It is God, not you Governor, who is really in charge. Pilate's response was that from that moment he sought to release Christ.

Any and all legitimate authority must trace its origin directly to God, for without that agency it is not legitimate. The authority which any king, president, congress, parliament or other civil body or figure holds over the governed comes from God. No matter how it may be structured or constituted the authority comes not from the consent of the governed, but rather the consent of God. Any genuine power in an economic relationship, such as employer-employee, is of a Divine derivation. The power that law enforcement wields must be traceable to God, as is the authority of parent over child. The history if this world should contain several volumes describing the misuse and abuse of authority by those who would wield it, and with such God has never been pleased.

Our study, though, is to be focused on Christ so the next natural inquiry concerns how He employed all this authority. Although Jesus was the source of all authority His life accented not authority, but ministry and sacrifice. He came not to provide a sternness of rule, a tyranny or a despotism, for the world has its share of those already. He came both literally and spiritually to provide Himself. It was Christ, who when tempted by Satan, provided those words as yet uncomprehended by most:

> "It is written, Man shall not live by bread alone, but by every word that proceedeth out of the mouth of God."

Literally did this ultimate "authority figure" provide that bread when at the Last Supper with His apostles He broke that bread and gave it to them saying:

> "This is my body which is given for you: this do in remembrance of Me."

The world yearns for substance, and it is given pablum, image and emptiness, while Christ provides the substance of life in giving his literal body for sacrifice. Earlier, He had taken bread beyond its literal meaning when He proclaimed that:

> "I am the bread of life: he that cometh to me shall never hunger; and he that believeth in me shall never thirst."

So many in all levels of authority or assumed authority promise change, alteration, transformation, a new world order, yet bring confusion, destruction and mayhem. So much authority has an aura of harshness, of demands, hardness and rigor, but the only true authority lived the only truly exemplary life of sacrifice, service and giving.

To complete this circle of substance God knows that all men and women, all of life itself, needs not only bread but water. The modern person in an advanced country is accustomed to water on demand and for all purposes, drinking, personal hygiene or recreation. The lands of the Bible, though, and especially the Judea in which Christ lived were dry places, devoid of abundance of water. Even the water that was available demanded an expenditure of time and effort to obtain, and while it is doubtful that many died of thirst it remained at a premium. Its acquisition and usage likely weighed daily on the minds of the people. One day Jesus was teaching at the Temple, the great edifice of worship to God and the central focus of the religious establishment's corruption and perversion of true religion. The priests and the Pharisees, by now in the main His bitter enemies sent soldiers to apprehend Him, yet they found Him not. Instead on the final day of the Feast of the Tabernacles He was heard pleading:

"If any man thirst, let him come unto me and drink.
He that believeth on me, as the scripture hath said, out
of his belly shall flow rivers of living water."

We call to remembrance too that shortly before this Jesus had
met a Samaritan woman at Jacob's well and asked her for a drink of
water. This woman, surprised but not intimidated by the boldness of
the young Jewish teacher expressed her shock that He would even
stoop to speak to a Samaritan. Out of love Jesus replied that if she had
known who He really was she would have volunteered the water and
received "living water" in return. Then, with the gift of language and
in extraordinary beauty of explanation Christ spoke to her:

"Whosoever drinketh of this water shall thirst again:

But whosoever drinketh of the water that I shall give
him shall never thirst; but the water that I shall give
him shall be in him a well of water springing up into
everlasting life."

It was integral to the teaching of the Master that if He were accepted and obeyed, the follower's needs in the temporal sphere and
in eternity would both be fulfilled. Surely it is no accident that He
offered Himself as both bread, or food, and water, all the sustenance
one needs. This figure asked not for offerings to Himself but literally
provided Himself as the offering, the answer to any and all questions.

In the last few verses of New Testament scripture in the Book of
Revelation Christ announced that:

"I am Alpha and Omega, the beginning and end, the
first and the last."

Nowhere did Christ better demonstrate the thorough completeness of His offering and ministry in His life's work and literal offering of Himself as atonement for sin. Yet even the best of Christians, the truest and most devoted retain vestiges of carnality and may be given to asking additional questions regarding Christ's nature. These questions and doubts, though, are minimalistic when placed beside those inquests of the doubter, the worldly, and the skeptic. As to Christ's claims to provide everything they may well say, "...but I have everything all ready." I live at a prosperous level which much of the world and almost all history would envy, so my earthly "bread and water" is already well supplied. As for the "spiritual" I live a reasonably decent and honest life, harm no one intentionally, and whatever deities there may be will surely smile favorably upon me and my life when the end of my days has come. What need I of the offerings of Jesus Christ?

The Son of God is rightfully established as the sole authority in all matters, especially those of which we term "religious." If He is the sole source of legitimate authority then why do the people who seriously follow Him number a relative few, for even as He remarked "...for many be called but few are chosen." The pretended authorities are many, or as Christ Himself might have said their numbers are "legion" and from many of them He received His most ferocious opposition, an embittered hatred that took Him to the cross. Jesus, above any man, recognized that in His day, in that short span of His earthly life, the Jewish people were in the spiritual death grip of sects and factions, each competing with the other but uniting in their contempt and hatred for the Messiah. To even the casual reader of the New Testament their names are quite familiar, Sadducee, scribe and Pharisee. Until literally the final week of His life the Sadducees, the priestly caste, were secondary to the scribes and Pharisees, and it is to them we will direct attention. The scribes were a class of scholars who transcribed, copied, taught and interpreted the Law of Moses for the people. They were considered the intellectual elite of the Jewish people, a self-flattering view which they did little to discourage. The Pharisees were the strictest of Jewish sects, admirable for the presumed serious and scrupulous attention to the Law but through the years becoming a short-sighted legalistic and harsh gate through which all Jews had to pass for spiritual approval. For three years these two groups were the constant companions of Jesus in His ministry, at times feigning respect but more often revealing their deep contempt and fear of Him. They argued, asked ridiculous questions on arcane points of the Law, and were a besetting woe to the Savior. Perhaps, though, their character and conduct had led them to reasons for their hatred of Jesus. Once Christ issued this caution to His disciples:

> "Beware, the leaven of the Pharisees, which is hypocrisy."

The terms "hypocrisy" and "hypocrite" are today thrown about with abandon, but we may note that in the entire Bible Christ is the only speaker who ever employed the terms. Yet He saw the falseness in the teaching of this sector of the religious establishment, and more strikingly did He condemn the scribe:

> "Beware of the scribes, which desire to walk in long robes, and love greetings in the markets, and the highest seats in the synagogues, and the chief rooms at feasts.
>
> Which devour widows' houses, and for a show make long prayers: the same shall receive greater damnation."

These two statements, both searing in their heat and intensity, were actually only a prelude to Christ's more extensive commentary on their presumed religious prominence and authority which He delivered only a few days before His arrest and trial.

For three years Christ had been subject to what we today would call harassment, with every sentence, every phrase, each action being parsed, criticized and questioned. Finally, this man who we aptly call the Prince of Peace, the Lamb of God and so gentle that He would not break a bruised reed turned on His accusers. Surprisingly, His first words were to acknowledge their authority because as He explained, "…the Pharisees sit in Moses's seat," but do not act or live as they do. In a phrase in which such behavior is often encapsulated, they did not "practice what they preached." Repeatedly, He condemned these self-appointed religious authorities for their hunger for recognition and the limelight, for the self-righteous showiness of their religion, which extended even to the clothes they wore and for the religious pretense and farce of extended public prayers said to prove their righteousness. Most of all, though, He with almost poetic repetition of "Woe unto you, scribes and Pharisees, hypocrites…" condemned them for the malice and evil which hid behind their cloaks of religious self-righteousness and authority. He excoriated them for sins which they doubtless believed had been well hidden, black marks such as extortion, fraud, iron-like rigidity of thinking and teaching in trivial doctrinal matters and a general lack of love or even concern for the people over whom they influenced and ruled. All a far cry from the one true Authority who sacrificed Himself at each step of the way, leading down the Way of Sorrows to the cross. No wonder they hated Him.

All these sects and their adherents are now consigned to the Bible, history books and theological works, for they are with us no more. With the fall and destruction of Jerusalem in 70 AD the entire

Jewish religious organization, its structure and assorted theological paraphernalia fell, never to rise again. The priesthood, the Pharisees and Sadducees and other assorted sects and cliques were silenced. So well may we ask the question of whether the study of them and their ongoing conflicts with Christ bear any but historical interest. Time, as always, has moved forward, Christ and Christianity have faced many foes, and a blinkered view would surely be that these Biblical conflicts, so brilliantly painted in the gospels, have faded into a dim historical curiosity. Seemingly, history and the Bible have shown an almost endless agenda of ways to be wrong religiously. Although as recognized entities and societal segments the Pharisees, Sadducees and scribes are gone their spirit lives in their spiritual descendants and heirs. The entire structure of many sectors of Christendom, from the deeply rooted historical hierarchy of Roman Catholicism and many "high church" Protestant denominations is likely as much an affront to Christ as was the Jewish religious establishment of His day. It is in the nature of man that large bureaucratic structures, be they political, military or religious attract swarms of place seekers and self servers, who in the guise of the religious authority seek to impose their views and what Christ called the "traditions of men" upon others. The Son of God came to break barriers between God and humanity, yet many still labor assiduously to construct as many obstacles between God and humanity as possible. Underlying it all is the presumption, even expressed openly by the Jewish leaders of the first century, that "we" the self-styled religious elite know best, and that "we" will stand in an interpretive and intercessory role between God and His presumably ill-equipped adherents. The spirit of "I am the Alpha and the Omega" the beginning and the end lives in any person or group, assembly, synod, council or other body which believes its judgment must be substituted for the simple teachings of Christ, the true Alpha and Omega. Yes, the spirit of Phariseeism, the religious exclusivity of the Sadducees, and the intellectual pretensions of the scribes live yet today. Their voices continually challenge the majesty of the true Authority, Jesus Christ.

Any honest, sincere analysis of the statement that "I am Alpha and Omega, the beginning and the end," compels the realization that on its face the declaration is preposterous. Literally this man is declaring that He is everything, and that apart from Him there is no meaning and no real existence. No one else had the audacity to proclaim that He and He along was the resurrection and the life, that He is the Way, the Truth and the Life and without Him a person effectively is "...dead while she liveth." A famous quotation from likely the greatest Christian apologist of modern times must now be offered. C. S. Lewis, upon a consideration of the whole of the life of Jesus and the many statements and claims He made for Himself must be take as either "...Lord, liar, or lunatic." The world has taken Him for all three, but the Christian obviously sees Him as Lord. To accept Him is to accept all of Him, all His teachings "even the hard sayings."

It is a relatively easy task for a person to sound authoritative, to look authoritative and to many seemingly even to radiate authority, to be the "be all" and "end all" in religious matters. It is self-flattering, thrilling, maybe even glorious to receive the plaudits and accolades of the crowd who proclaim the preacher, teacher or speaker as a "gift from God," such a great man or woman and one whose knowledge, wisdom and life itself transcends the mundane of the mediocrity. How warm the emotions and hearts must be of those who Jesus said love "...the greetings in the markets and to called of men Rabbi, Rabbi." All of this the common currency of so much religious practice, first or twenty-first vintage. It is so noticeable, so celebratory, so self-congratulatory and so cheap.

How much more difficult yet how much more real it was to be the true Alpha and Omega, to be the authority who held children in His arms, the same arms that had long wielded carpentry tools to earn a living by the sweat of His brow. What real substance there proved to be in a man who stood upright against powerful, entrenched opposition and who taught and spoke against every evil. The reality of this Authority is that He was on His hands and knees just a few hours before His arrest, trial and crucifixion washing the feet of His disciples, employing those same hands into which rugged, jagged nails would soon be driven. Truly He is the Alpha and Omega, and wisely did God say:

"Hear ye Him."

{ 8 }

MASTER

The informality of the twenty-first century has demanded an informality in names. Older, more stable and staid societies saw their members speaking to one another in terms of respect and even deference. The constant exchange of Mr., Mrs., and Miss, even among persons who had known each other and even worked together closely for years emitted an aura of a combined respectability, artificiality and even quaintness. For the present, though, these times are a historical novelty and curiosity never experienced by the young and of fading memory to the old. All is now on a first name basis, between employer and employee, sometimes between teacher and student and remarkably between parent and child. The wisdom and advisability of this we leave to other commentators, but it provides an interesting and contrasting backdrop for the fact that the four gospels of the New Testament reflect not a single instance where the son of May and Joseph was addressed by His friends with His given name of Jesus. That He was called such by friends and family while a child and a youth there can be little doubt. Yet those closest to Him, especially for the final three years of His life, the apostles, other close disciples, both men and women, employed one term far above all when addressing Him, Master. Over thirty times is this address found, and it was seemingly employed with the same ease and grace which we utilize first names with family and friends. For Master is sometimes substituted the title Rabbi, but regardless they both mean the same, that being "Teacher." To the Jews no higher accolade existed than to be considered a Master or great teacher. As a people they strongly emphasized (and still do today) the importance of education and knowledge. To be recognized as a great exemplar and purveyor of that knowledge as a teacher was indeed noteworthy. Christ is certainly worthy of all the nomenclature with which he has been provided, yet few titles are more befitting to Him than that of Master. No other human who has ever lived could be known by some of Hit titles, such as Prince of Peace, Lamb of God or the Resurrection and the Life, yet many are masters or teachers, even of religious matters. Jesus, though, was not just a good or even great teacher, a wise authority or merely masterful with His words. Singularly, He is the Master, the sole source of authority. Many men and women by their knowledge, ability and dedication have given great honor to the teaching profession, and many have not. In His manner and doctrines, though, Christ so shone that we may assert that teachers fall into one of two categories, (1) the first is Christ Himself and (2) everyone else. What were those qualities that engendered such love and respect that individuals gratefully and easily called Him Master? Most are easy to discern, but as with any study of Christ and His teachings the deeper the depths we fathom the more we find.

History's most famous public address occurred in no legislative or Parliamentary forum, and neither was it delivered in the small town of Gettysburg, Pennsylvania. Its location was an unknown hill in Judea in the first century, at which a multitude of interested listeners had gathered in the early stages of Jesus's ministry. We know it as the Sermon on the Mount, three short chapters of the distilled essence of truth itself delivered by a man who Himself was Truth. As His words clearly demonstrated Christ knew what was on the minds of those who had gathered to hear Him, and He saw before Him a collection of humanity, for all of whom He had sympathy and respect. His first words reflected just how much respect and understanding for He began:

> "Blessed are the poor in spirit: for theirs is the Kingdom of heaven."

As a teacher Jesus always knew His audience, whether it be a multitude or a single man or woman, and always did He speak to them with understanding and respect. This was not a gathering of the rich and famous, but of humble, supposedly ordinary people, perhaps humble by nature or even humbled by life experience. This, His first words bless them for their humility and point them to Heaven's path. He continued in this same vein with eight more blessings, or Beatitudes. Christ knew that primarily His followers would be gathered from that endless stream of "common" people which the world supplies, and not from the prideful and self-sufficient. His words, appropriate to all, were always especially fitted to the audience of His immediate message.

Just as frequently, though, if not more so, the students standing in His presence held deep hostility for Him as a person, as a "pretended" Messiah and for His doctrines. They continually devised traps of words, examples and even living human beings as kinds of bait to ensnare and destroy Him. An oft-cited story is of the woman taken in adultery, in the "very act" thereof. One morning Jesus was quietly teaching in the Temple, when a commotion arose as a group of scribes and Pharisees burst in, interrupting His lesson as they hurled before Him a young woman taken in adultery. They challenged Him with the incisive comment that the Mosaiacal Law demanded death for adultery, but they wanted His opinion on the subject. For the only time of which we are given knowledge Jesus responds to them, although it be transitory, with the written word. He stooped down and wrote with His finger in the dirt. For two thousand years His writing has been the subject of all types of speculation and scholarship, although to this day we may only surmise by its effects. He rose from the ground and spoke words which are still quoted often out of context but cited nonetheless:

> "He that is without sin among you, let him first cast
> a stone."

He stooped down again and continued writing. One by one, commencing with the eldest, these men "…being convicted by their own conscience" walked away and left the woman along with the Savior. He cautioned her of the dangers of the sin of adultery, but condemned her not, and she went on her way. This story is rightfully cited as a treasure trove of teachings on many moral subjects such as the perils of adultery, improper judging, lack of feeling and ultimately forgiveness. Almost always overlooked is the relationship between Christ and His bitter foes, the scribes and the Pharisees.

Is it often supposed, with likely reason, that Jesus enumerated the sins of these men, starkly and one by one when He wrote on the ground. Would it not have been easier to simply speak what He had written to the scribes and Pharisees? Most assuredly it would have been, but these men, albeit their motives were malicious, would not have been able to retire gracefully from this scene. Today, the bitterness of normal discourse between many persons has become cruder and more vituperative. An ugly phrase, employed commonly in the political area, is that one person "destroyed" another with his/her arguments. Jesus, the Son of God, the true Master never sought to destroy any person. As He told His apostles:

> "The Son of man is come to seek and save that which is lost."

Christ called all, including scribes and Pharisees, to repentance, although most never came. He had respect and love for their souls, however, and knew that a man who has been held to public ridicule and humiliation is unlikely to ever become a disciple. The Master had no interest in winning arguments, in making debating points or the "gotcha" style of pseudo-debate which is so common in the media age. He was interested in lost souls, not in sarcasm towards a detractor. It did not always work, but sometimes it did. The scribes and Pharisees remained enemies and were integral elements in the conspiracy to crucify Christ. Not all, though. Some, as many of the priests as well, later became Christians. Even His fiercest opponent, the self-described 'Pharisee of the Pharisees," Saul of Tarsus, changed and became the greatest evangelist in history, the apostle Paul.

Jesus was unsurpassed as the Master in his ability to get students involved in the lesson, sometimes even those (perhaps especially) that were dismissive of His message. A good, even a minimally competent, teacher continually poses hypotheticals and asks questions. A teacher who is content to merely lecture is no real teacher, but in fact is just that, a lecturer. Christ had a superlative talent to draw in the listener to the extent that he became not just a listener, but a participant.

Once while He was teaching Christ was confronted by the boldness of a lawyer, who sought not just knowledge but "tempted" Christ, hopefully into an answer upon which he could pounce. He posed to Christ the query:

"Master, what shall I do to inherit eternal life?"

Adeptly Christ responds with a question, the answer to which doubtlessly was already known by the lawyer:

"What is written in the law? how readest thou?"

In these more prosaic times but in language any lawyer should understand effectively he asks him "what does the record say," which impels him to answer his own question in this manner:

"Thou shalt love the Lord thy God with all thy heart, and with all thy soul, and with all thy strength, and with all thy mind and thy neighbor as thy self."

As a teacher Christ has shown himself as beyond mere mortal brilliance. With a minimum of dialogue and using only scripture He has turned the lawyer's question upon himself and effectively compelled him to answer his own question. For but a moment both the Master and the pupil "look good" but the young lawyer cannot leave well enough alone. "Willing to justify himself" he cannot help but push Christ one step further with the query "And who is my neighbor?" The response of Christ is likely both instructive and self-devastating to the lawyer, as Jesus responds with one of the most famous stories in history, the Parable of the Good Samaritan, which forever hence has set the standard for defining and loving a neighbor.

Not all question and answer sessions were with His detractors and in fact more are to be found in His relationships with His disciple. On an earlier day Jesus was with His apostles, walking along the coasts of

Caesarea Philippi, where idols and images of pagan gods were plentiful. This time the Master begins the questions with the simple "Whom do men say that I the son of man am." They respond with a briefing of many identities, from the great ancient prophets such as Elijah and Jeremiah to the most recent herald, John the Baptist. His follow up question elicits from Peter the most important answer ever given. "But whom say ye that I am," prompting Peter's response:

"Thou are the Christ, the Son of the living God."

Into the hills along Caesarea's coasts were implanted stone sculptures of the Greek and Roman deities, cold, dead monuments that the apostle Peter joyfully contrasted with a Savior who was the son of the "living" God. The teaching of Jesus was truly masterful, for He has made no declaratory sentences and instead offered only too short, simple questions. Nonetheless the point was made, and the foundational stone for Christianity was laid.

His group of apostles, though, were His key followers, those that were with Him in body and in spirit and who served as the foundation of the church. With short questions and short answers, He could also lay eternal principles in His confrontations with His most bitter enemies.

First century Judea was a political powder keg. On the far eastern fringes of the Roman Empire, this small community, a mere sliver of land was a continuing headache to its masters in far away Rome. The Jews highly resented the foreign presence and were divided into competing sects, many of whom would gladly slice any Roman throat within reach. The Romans were keenly aware of this and exercised vigilance and diligence and when necessary savagely suppressed any sign of rebellion from the conquered Jews. As Christ's earthly days were growing few in number the murderous conspiracy against Him began to coalesce. Two of the chief conspiracy partners were the scribes and most importantly and publicly the chief priests, who were Sadducees. Together they sought to entrap this upstart Master with a question that could not be satisfactorily or safely answered and the posing of this inquiry puts a glaring spotlight on the actions and motives of all.

Their self-introduction to the Savior set a standard for sarcastic unctuousness that has yet to be equaled:

> "Master, we know that sayest and teachest rightly,
> neither acceptest thou the person of any, but teachest
> the way of God truly."

What a repellant, hypocritical introduction for the question they sense will finally ensnare Jesus and reveal Him as either a blasphemer or an enemy of the Romans:

> "Is it lawful for us to give tribute until Caesar or no?"

Jesus "perceiving their craftiness" asked for a Roman coin and made further inquiry of it:

> "Whose image and superscription hath it?"

Truthfully, they answered "Caesar's." With one sentence the Master answered them and gave the imprimatur for all church-state relations forever:

> "Render therefore unto Caesar the things which be
> Caesar's, and unto God the things which be God's."

This one sentence and its reach and deepest meaning provides more theological and political theory than libraries of volumes which human philosophers have penned. Pay taxes to the state, unhesitatingly answered Christ. Caesar is powerful, is ordained by God, but his power and the State's authority is definitely held within the temporal sphere. All other matters and a person's ultimate allegiance is claimed by God. Much more may be written of this, but further words and phrases would likely mar the beauty of the lesson's brevity. All this teaching was done with one short question and one brief answer. Truly, He is the Master.

One elemental quality in much teaching often is omitted from discussion, glossed over or just completely ignored, and that is the factor of boredom. Many lessons, sermons, lectures and other public presentations are often stultified by boredom, and this subject is not easily bounded. It would be the rare person who has never sat in a stuffy classroom and endured a boring lecture from a teacher, or in a church and been subjected to a well-meaning preacher, minister or priest. These assertions make allowance that many people are often bored because they are boring people, with a limited range of interests and beset with dull minds. Boredom, though, is not the province of these alone, for many seek mental stimulation in any and all subjects, some even in religion. The hard fact is that multitudes of teachers, preachers and speakers are boring. The Bible reveals many reactions to the teachings of Christ, astonishment, love, bewilderment, hatred, even confusion, but it reveals not a single instance of boredom. He captivated immediately any audience, be it a single man or woman, a small group or a multitude. As a teacher did the Master have a special secret? No doubt He possessed abilities no other man could claim, and among those was His Divinely intuitive grasp of what troubled the minds of His listeners. Again, we turn our gaze to the most cited of all His teachings, the Sermon on the Mount.

A quick, very abbreviated inventory of the topics which Christ addressed in this masterful work include anger, various marital issues between husbands and wives, improper sexual desire and lust, religious phonies and hypocrites, money worries, materialism and concerns about the future. Which of these topics is passé, dated and no longer of any interest? They held a university of interest that knits together all eras, cultures, races, both sexes and all ages because they are the sum and substance of ordinary living, and none knew this more than the Master. When He spoke to a person or a crowd, He knew what was on the minds of the audience and what worries and temptations with which each was contending. He was not as the scribes and Pharisees, for as Matthew related, He "…taught them as one having authority." No man no woman can approach the insight which Christ, the Son of God, possessed, but His manner is a template of methodology for all teachers. He could have come to each and participated in the theological hair-splitting disputes of the religious establishment and clergy. The Master turned from that and pivoted towards the issue of daily living, true morality and how God may truly be served. None were accustomed to this teaching, and again as Matthew related, they were "astonished." Every word the Master spoke that day of the Judean hillside remains just as astonishing.

No real adult, no serious person, and even children should ever be enticed by a steady diet of fluff. In writing one of his Biblical epistles the apostle Paul admonished certain believers that whereas they should be hungry for the "meat" of the word their desire was yet for milk. In the modern world, even Christendom, if we continue to employ the metaphor of food and drink for teaching, most people are being fed a steady diet of junk food. While the Jews of Jesus's day were being force fed legalism, rules and rigidity more often now our presumed Christian masters serve sweet dishes of self-acceptance, self- esteem and, though, it rarely goes by this appellation self-importance. Harshness, legalism and burdensome religious teaching is non-Biblical but so also is an unending diet of pablum.

The form, the manner and the style of Christ's teaching was unequaled and certainly unsurpassed, but it is the substance of His words upon which we right fully focus. Jesus had such an immediate and a lasting impact that many people, with well meaning intentions, assume that He introduced new doctrines, a new system of religion and a religious revolution. Actually, He did not. What the Master did was to strip away centuries upon centuries of religious tradition, authoritative doctrines from teachers who really had no authority and divisions in thinking that were driven by an extreme sectarian spirit of many. In His own words Jesus came not to destroy the Law, but rather to "fulfill" it. His teachings were meant to be revolutionary, but the revolution was not against any earthly government or power but rather a revolution in the heart of each man and woman. The Master's teaching was the apogee of understanding and explanation as to what His Father meant; not what people had themselves determined He meant.

In offering a deeper understanding of truth Christ knew what all great writers and storytellers have always known, and that is a realization that the subject most interesting to human beings is the story of other human beings. Other than the aptly named Sermon on the Mount the gospels record few examples where Christ actually preached a sermon. His favorite and most prolific mode of public (and often private) teaching was in His utilization of short stories which have come down to us as parables. The brief gospel accounts alone reveal dozens of these, all of brevity and some as short as a mere two or three verses. All are populated by persons, often in ordinary situations, with common and normal family connections and ordinary human relation-ships. We have noted that of the Good Samaritan and to that most famous of stories we add those of the Prodigal Son, the Talents, the Sower, the rich man and Lazarus or on He went. Each story was un-canny in its offering and presentation of real characters, at least one of whom each listener could relate and sense a common bond. In allegor-ical form they told of the joys, pains, drudgeries and satisfactions of everyday living by ordinary people. In an often-over-employed term, they are "relevant," relevant, pertinent to the lives of first century Jew of a twenty-first century American and to anyone else we could add to the mix. This teacher, the one and only true Master, expressed in His simple words a depth of understanding of the joys and vicissitudes of life to which no other teacher has ever remotely approached.

In closing this brief review of Jesus as the Master perhaps the most remarkable element of the marvelous epic story of His masterful teaching is the economy of His word usage. All have been plagued by being subjected to the endless droning, run-on sentence, duplicated examples and the general ennui of so many teachers, whether aca-demic or religious. These are the instructors who seem to follow as their guiding star a principle of always using at least ten words where one will serve better. Look at the true Master, who has given us an abundance of brevity and an economy of words, which along capture our attention. Consider briefly three platinum plated examples. When His apostle Philip asked Jesus to see His Father Christ replied that "If you have seen me you have seen the Father," thereby in one short sen-tence establishing the perfect unbreakable unity of Father and Son. So powerful is this bond that Christ expressed the exclusivity of the path of God in fewer words than any of these sentences use:

"No man cometh to the Father but by me."

Yet the most beautiful and succinct message which the Master delivered was in a moment of great grief when He came to His dear friends, the sisters Martha and Mary, as they were awash in tears over the sudden death of their brother Lazarus. When Jesus assured Martha, that Lazarus would be raised from the dead Martha's recognition of this fact was met by the closest to a one sentence encapsulation of truth as was ever spoken:

> "I am the resurrection and the life; he that believeth in
> me, though he were dead, yet shall he live. And who-
> soever liveth and believeth in me shall never die."

Master of the elements, Master of words, Master of any situation, He truly is the one Master.

{ 9 }

MAN OF SORROWS

It is so easy and enticing to think of Jesus walking among an adoring multitude of eager, even excited men and women, children striving and straining to get near Him. Likely a few small animals, maybe cats and lambs help populate this throng of happy disciples, with the happiest of all being Jesus Himself, beckoning, smiling and emitting a magnetism never seen before or since. With a certainty these were all true representations of scenes in the life of Christ. Less well known and publicized are certain other images of this man, faded with the passage of years, not as attractive and apparently consigned to historical and religious memory holes. How few people remember and how many have forgotten that the Savior was aptly described by the prophet Isaiah as a "…man of sorrows, and acquainted with grief." It is so much more pleasant to portray Him as a happy Messiah, walking in sunlight, birds chirping and surrounded by the spectacular bloom of flowers. It is a distraction, perhaps even repugnant to an artificially constructed image of Him to view Him weeping at the death of those

He loved, groaning in His spirit, immersed in the soul searing torment of Gethsemane and the blood-borne pains of Calvary.

It is a time honored but well-worn cliché to express in varying form that each life has its share of sorrows, or more poetically "... into each life some rain must fall." It is to minimize the number and depths of His sorrows to state only that Christ was no exception. His short earthly walk was filled with more sorrows of a greater variety and reaching depths still unfathomed by any other man or woman. Christ experienced sorrows at a human level with which few persons have any familiarity, but as the Son of God the pains and afflictions which beset Him were greater than any other man could bear, and to an extent that only His Divine nature could comprehend. Not all of His sorrows, though, are beyond our ken, and in fact many were of the sort and nature that most of humanity experiences.

A sorrow which to some degree is shared by many is the recognition that to many who knew or should have known Him best He was nothing special. Well summarized is this fact in a single statement from John, the apostle:

> "He came unto His own, and His own received Him not."

Jesus grew up in the small non-descript village of Nazareth close to the Sea of Galilee. From the limited information available to us it appears that except for his first five years of His life when He lived in Egypt Nazareth was His home. Little if anything in the gospels indicates that He was looked upon as anything special, except for one reference wherein Luke states that "...Jesus increased in wisdom, and stature and in favor with God and man." He thus attained a position for which all decent men and women still aspire, that is to live an honorable life and to be well respected. But something special? The

Savior of the world? The promised Messiah? Not hardly, for He, like His father was only a carpenter. Jesus came from a family of at least seven children, Himself and four brothers, James, Joseph, Simon and Judas, all common Jewish names and at least two sisters, identified in the plural but unnamed. At least during His lifetime His authority as the Son of God was rejected by His siblings. To put it mildly sibling relations, even the best of them, are often delicate flowers easily harmed and even crushed by various events. No more is said of this personal rejection, but the heartache suffered by Jesus is easily imagined.

The sorrows of the Savior were multiplied when He discovered quite early in His ministry that He would be no "favorite son" of the town of Nazareth, for the townspeople themselves so rejected Him that effectively He moved to the nearby village of Cana, which became the focal point of much of His effort and where many of His first disciples and even apostles were found. Well did the scripture state that "His own received Him not." The Son of God who came from Heaven was laden with the sorrow of having no real residence in the world which He had created.

Rejection is close to the nadir of all emotions which human beings are called upon to process. For many it starts early with a child's real or effective rejection by his own mother and/or father. Normal growth takes us all through childhood and youth, and the feelings of not being accepted or failed friendships help mold the character. The maturing of age most often brings great joy, even ecstasy, at finding the right person for life, for the hollow emotions of rejection from one who is loved and desired inflict pain and suffering to an extreme degree. Jesus knew individual rejection, a family's giving Him the brushoff and an entire hometown rising in clamorous opposition to Him. He also experienced the rejection and the opposition of an entire people and nation, the Jewish people. Of course He had Jewish disciples and all His apostles were His countrymen, but as a whole nation the Jewish people, the chosen ones, the recipients of the great promise given to Abraham, and those whom God had nourished through thick and thin were not only indifferent but often openly hostile. And how Jesus did know and feel this pain and sorrow continually. A poet was remarked that "there is nothing so sad as unrequited love." No love was greater than that which Christ had for the Jews, and His pain and sorrow were intensified when He realized just how much they needed Him for:

"They are like sheep without a shepherd."

Nowhere is the expression of the sorrow of His heart wrenching agony of rejection better expressed or more commonly cited than, just days before His crucifixion He looked upon the City of David, the heart of Judaism, and:

"O Jerusalem, Jerusalem, thou that killest the prophets, and stonest them which are sent unto thee, how often would I have gathered they children together, even as a hen gathereth her chickens under her wings, but ye would not!"

Words such as those delivered in the time and setting of the climatic moment to which events were careening were unlikely to be delivered in a bland monotone. The emotions and demeanor of Christ, the sorrows and regrets He suffered, are more to be imagined than described.

So much sorrow is derived not only from how things are but also from how we wish they could be. No human has suffered or even had the ability to suffer such grief as did Jesus from the moment He became the Son of Man and came to earth. All of us can read of how things were in the Edenic Paradise before the Fall of Man, but Jesus knows how they were. He was literally "present at the Creation" for He was part of the creative impetus. Christ knew, even as His tired feet tread the shores of Galilee or some dusty by-way just how far humanity had fallen from the perfection of Eden. He knew how lush and verdant was the entire earth before the ground itself was cursed. Perhaps most importantly He knew what a world was like before the entrance of the ever present dark spectre of death. Christ saw the plants and vegetation that struggled to spring from so much of the dry, dusty earth of Judea, and He knew this was not His Father's intention. He knew that it was meant to last forever, that plants, vegetation and flowers were not originally created to wither and die and be trampled and forgotten but to be as the poet John Keats wrote "a thing of beauty," and "a joy forever."

Moreover, and more importantly He was attuned to the life and death cycles of all living things, including animals. Christ noticed animals and spoke of them constantly, the overall effect of His speech leaving the obvious conclusion that they were dear to Him. He spoke of sparrows, foxes, fowls of the air, chickens, lions, cattle endlessly and all with an affectionate respect. How his earthly heart and heavenly soul must have grieved when He witnessed the quick extinguishment of the few years of life allotted to each. He saw and knew, and still does, the genuine agony which anyone who has ever loved a pet experiences upon the demise of the beloved companion and friend.

Yet it was His fellow men and women that Christ saw grief and sadness and experienced deep reservoirs of sorrow. He saw what disease and injury could wreak on the human body and how people and their families suffered with fevers, plagues, distorted and useless limbs and ravaged faces. Worst of all He was well and thoroughly experienced with the sorrows and woes suffered by the dying and even more so by those who had to witness them perish. Our only specific reference to His crying was when He was pained by the tears of His dear friend Mary, which had just lost her brother Lazarus. All said it would require a heart of iron to deny that this man Jesus of Nazareth saw and experienced firsthand a wealth of sorrows and His concern for the one whose lives He touched was great. But, queries the skeptic, does not any decent person sympathize with the afflicted? Was Jesus really that different than any other good man?

His earthly lifespan was short and abbreviated, a mere thirty-three years, but He lives yet and His concerns for His disciples have remained as real and intense as ever. As the writer of the great epistle of Hebrews proclaimed:

> "But we have not a high priest which cannot be touched with the feeling of our infirmities…"

Yes, resounding eternally so, He is still keenly aware of human suffering and especially while on earth must His sadness and sorrow been intensified by His knowledge that none of it was ever intended by God. God had created His perfect, innocent paradise, yet within the Edenic borders lurked a serpent which brought to the world the source of all human suffering and sorrow, disobedience and death. Surrounded by illness, disability, pain, death and grief Jesus knew that its source and His only real enemy was Satan, the great master and purveyor of death. We can only imagine Eden and Heaven, but Christ knows it. We can only imagine and see the results of Satan, but Christ knows him.

Few are the numbers who crave or even like opposition. The average, normal temperament warms to friendliness, courtesy and good will and seeks to avoid controversy and friction. In simple terms the disagreeable are not pleasant, and we certainly prefer those with whom we share a commonality of belief and outlook. The Son of God, though, had no such luxury, and for three years He bore a hurricane and hailstorm of embittered hateful opposition that would have given no one pleasure. Those who should have been the first to receive Him, even before His family and His fellow Nazarenes were His most ferocious opponents. The Jewish people prized learning especially religious learning and they possessed a hierarchical priesthood and sectarian factions such as the Sadducees and Pharisees who joined with the religious instructors, the scribes, all claimed preeminence in learning and meanings of the Law of Moses. The knowledge, both in depth and expanse, of many was awe inspiring. These, though, were the ones who pursued a dogged trail of opposition and verbal harassment of Jesus for a trial of years, giving Him opportunities to teach but doubtless heavily weighing on His heart that the most thoroughly schooled, the elite, were such hateful, implacable foes.

For three years as each day dawned undoubtedly like most persons Jesus had in His mind an itinerary, or at least an outline of what His day would be. Always there was the teaching, whether individually, in small groups or to the multitude. Most likely travel would be an element, for although Christ did not travel far, He did travel often. Personal teaching, instruction, commiseration and just friendship with His apostles were all elemental to His daily life. So was opposition, not merely disagreement, not only probing intelligent questions but fierce enmity from those who felt they had the most to lose from His ministry and Messiahship. In the latter stages of the gospels one man clearly expressed their collective fears when He voiced concern that because of Jesus they would lose their "station." All mature adults realize that not every day will be a smooth silken road to pleasure and happiness. We expect interruption and obstacles, and if they are not too overbearing, we process and handle them. This, though, is not the description of Jesus's days. Organized opposition from the intellectual and religious aristocracy, planned snares and entrapments and vitriolic personal assaults were part of the fabric of His daily life. One Pharisaical detractor called Christ, the Savior of the World, a descendant of Beelzebub, the devil. He was continually accused of ignoring the Law of Moses, where in actuality, He, the only man who ever perfectly obeyed the Law, was violating the Law itself. He was a Sabbath breaker because He did good and healed on the Sabbath, until Christ silenced them on this issue with the rejoinder that the Sabbath was made for man, not man for the Sabbath.

As vicious and bitter as was all this opposition to His teachings, it was likely surpassed by their continual employment of what we now call the argument ad hominem, which really means an attack on not the teaching but upon the person himself. Nothing was beyond the venom of the Pharisees and scribes, and at times their hatred for Him displayed embarrassingly their own ignorance. No time was more evident or noticeable than when His place of origin was incorrectly assumed to be Galilee. Galilee, of course, the northern section of the ancient Kingdom of Israel was a cultural backwater and snobbishly rejected and taunted by the self-designated sophisticates of Judea, of which Jerusalem was the center and capital. Jesus and His closest disciples were Galileans, and it naturally showed in their dress and roughly accented speech. A Judean intellect, a Pharisee or scribe from Jerusalem was not accustomed to being lectured or instructed by an itinerant backwoods upstart from Judea, and this was thrown in the face of Jesus:

> "Art thou also of Galilee? Search, and look: for out of
> Galilee ariseth no prophet."

Well and bravely spoken except the accusation has an untruth for its foundation. Jesus arose not from Galilee but rather Bethlehem, the famous small Judean village.

It was not His birthplace or origins alone for which they attempted to pillory Jesus. In fact, this was secondary to a larger truth that gnawed at His detractors, that clouded their thinking on every issue and seemingly drove them almost to madness in their animus for Him. He was not one of "them". He was a carpenter, dressed plainly, from a non-descript rural outpost, and what's more He lacked what we now often call "credentials." Jesus could claim no great formal education and He did not grow to maturity tutored by the finest of Jewish scholars, men esteemed even today, scholars such as Hillel or Gamaliel. Likely His primary earthly educators were His parents, Mary and Joseph, each of whom was bereft of recognized formal educational authority. This mental and moral posturing reached its zenith when the chief priests and Pharisees denigrated Him by saying:

"Are ye also deceived?

Have any of the rulers or of the Pharisees believed in Him?"

For intellectual and moral arrogance and insularity it is doubtful that this declaration will ever be bested. It is a heartfelt expression of the deeply held beliefs of the ruling clique, the expression of an emotion and a disease which runs rampant in the world, perhaps most prevalently in the modern age. Every nation, every people, every university, all societies, our oppressive media and entertainment culture, the academy and religion still is rife with the oppressive self-appointed cliques which determine "truth." Jesus, the Son of God, faced the purest expression of this phenomenon.

All that we have here noted are frequently told stories and employed regularly in the Christian canon of teaching to illustrate both wrong and the opposition which Jesus fought. Throughout it all, though, it is easy to overlook the emotion of sadness and sorrows which this Man of Sorrows endured. Let it be remembered that in spite of their ferocity, the ugliness of their character and action, and the acidic vitriol which they daily threw upon Him, Christ loved these men, just as He loves all, even the closest and purest of His disciples. The pangs of His emotional torture when daily He had to engage in combat with men who should have been His most eager followers, but as He later said on that hill overlooking Jerusalem, "…they would not."

As great and devastating as may be the opposition the hatred and animosity from those who oppose us, a feeling shared, at least some degree by all humanity, it pales in comparison to the agonies, mental and moral tribulations which may be inflicted upon us by our friends and family. This, too, is likely an emotional experience of all humanity. Earlier we noted the rejection of Jesus by His brothers and sisters, yet the scriptures indicate that at least in part this was resolved. The opening chapter of the Book of Acts references His "brethren" as being assembled with the apostles and other disciples. Whether this is inclusive of all his brothers and sisters is speculative, but we know that James, the brother of Jesus, became one of the prominent leaders of the early Church and the author of the epistle that bears his name.

Thankfully Christ had many early disciples, and the overwhelming majority appear to have remained true in their loyalties. He had twelve particular disciples, personally selected by Him and given the highest honors imaginable. These apostles were to be the foundation of the Church itself, and among those so highly honored was Judas Iscariot. These men spent a three-year apostolic apprenticeship in the company and under the instruction of the Son of God Himself, an education never to be surpassed by any. Everything in the gospel accounts indicates that Judas was fully accepted by all, so much so that he was the treasurer of the group. In any society, ancient or modern, entrusting a person with money is a high compliment indeed. In His few recorded exchanges with Jesus nothing shows that Jesus singled him out in any way. Men will not voluntarily associate themselves with other men for a period of three years unless there exists a bond, a camaraderie and a friendship with an easy exchange of words and opinions. Although Peter was the most prominent and John personally the closest to the Master, in no sense were they greater in importance than Judas. The name Judas, though, highly esteemed and elevated at the outset, has long been the most toxic name in our language and a synonym for that most odious of persons, a traitor. Doubtless anyone reading these words is thoroughly versed in the tragedy of Judas Iscariot, complete with the revelation of his being a common thief and embezzler, His betrayal with a kiss of the Son of Man for thirty pieces of silver, and his ignominious end when he hanged himself. Long has he justly borne the scorn and opprobrium of history. But what of Christ, the betrayal? The story of His Passion, His death, burial and resurrection is the central core of Christianity, but what was the emotional harm to Jesus as a man, the Man of Sorrows? Judas was a man He lived with travelled the rough roads of Galilee, Samaria and Judea, shared meals, cold and heat, discomfort, sadness and laughter. Surely among the pains which Christ carried to the Cross was the searing agony of a disciple's and friend's betrayal.

Like everything else in this world all the sorrows of the Son of Man are temporal, and their lifespan ends when the curtain is lowered on this mortal sphere. Christ, as we see from this brief work, lays claim to so many titles which are descriptive of His character and personality. In eternity He is still the Good Shepherd, Wonderful,

Counselor, the Light of the World which now lights the eternal day of the afterlife. No longer, though, will He be the Man of Sorrows. The King we will then view is the King of Heaven, a place more marvelous and beautiful than Eden a home where:

> "God shall wipe away all tears from our eyes: and there shall be no more death, neither sorrow, nor crying, neither shall there by any more pain: for the former things are passed away."

The bad, the drudgery, the pain, the heartaches, the goodbyes, will all be gone and forgotten. No wonder is it that the beloved apostle John closes the Bible with the petition to Christ:

> "Even so, come, Lord Jesus."

{ 10 }

THE LAMB OF GOD

Lambs are innocent, so innocent that historically and culturally they have always been symbols and synonymous with the word itself. In our modern urbanized society few persons have experienced actual hands on dealings with these young fresh-faced sheep, but it is a hardened heart that is not affected by the sight or visage of a lamb. Little imagination is needed to understand how and why the phrase "innocent as a lamb" has worked its way into our language. Although no such statement is ever made in the Bible it would be difficult to argue that the lamb has not always held a special place in God's Creation. With no other guides than the scriptures themselves they alone provide ample evidence that so much of the Biblical, especially the Old Testament world, was a great and fertile region for raising sheep.

The Old Testament records many of its foremost characters to have been herders of sheep, or rather "shepherds," among whom is the illustrious roster of Abraham, Isaac, Jacob, Moses and as a youth David, in his own way perhaps the man most associated with sheep and lambs. Lambs were born, raised, nurtured and shepherded, providing

the living for many. Although the flesh of the animal was eaten oc-
casionally their primary value was their wool. They were the liveli-
hood for many and have given the world more imagery, metaphor and
allegorical narratives than any other animal. So vital and entwined in
literature and the scriptural story they are that the voice of the narrator
in the most famous of all Psalms and perhaps the most quoted poem
ever written, the 23rd Psalm, is that of a lamb, who declares "The
Lord is my Shepherd..." and proceeds to exalt his own shepherd for
His love and tender caring. It is no accident (for accidents are non-
existent with God) that the author of this Psalm was King David, a
former shepherd boy. David intimately knew the work of a shepherd,
and as much as is given to any person he understood what it meant to
be a lamb, their fears, struggles and even joys. David, as purely and
surely as any person who ever lived, knew that he looked into the
purity of innocence when he gazed into the face of a lamb. He doubtless realized that the lamb's countenance reflected the goodness and
Divine satisfaction greater than did that of any sinful man or woman.

A long and often torturous road stretched from David's pastoral
boyhood days when he watched over his father's sheep to a rooftop
in Jerusalem decades later when he as an apparently firmly ensconced
King of Israel began a relationship with Bathsheba, murdered a good
and honorable man, enticed the King himself into traitorous conduct
and came within a hair's breadth of destroying his life and character.
This story, one of the most noted in the Bible, requires no further
detailed retelling, but suffice it to record that King David apparently
has triumphed. He retains the throne, Uriah the lawful husband is in
his grave, and David now has the young, beautiful Bathsheba as his
wife. All is right in David's world. It is not right with God, though,
who dispatches the prophet Nathan to spring a surprise upon the King.
Nathan's narrative describes a very rich man who hosts a banquet for

a traveler into his city. Instead of selecting from the vastness of his own herds he takes the one lamb owned by a poor man in the same city, an innocent lamb so dear to its owner that it "…was unto him as a daughter." The wealthy man slaughters the lamb, and David's ire is kindled to white hot intensity until Nathan fells him with the immortal words of "Thou art the man." David, a one-time gentle shepherd youth but now a mature man who has waded through streams of blood with his own hands besmeared with the clotted blood of his foes has his heart touched by the willful slaying of an innocent lamb. It is indeed remarkable that God knows the imagery which will penetrate the hearts of men and women.

In Nathan's story the innocent lamb was slaughtered, and ever since lambs in countless multitudes have been killed for food and for religious sacrifice. All did so unknowingly and unwillingly with a singular exception, Jesus Christ. He, the eternal Lamb of God willingly offered His life as a sacrifice for sin, and most Christians accept and understand this central truth of Christianity. When we think of His sacrifice our thoughts and eyes are pointed to the Cross on Calvary, and well they should. Yet our Savior, our sacrificial lamb, offered the entirety of His life, not just the terminus of His death, in sacrifice for us.

From the opening chapters of Genesis wherein the drama in Eden unfolds the desirability and the essentiality of sacrifice and self-denial is extolled as a requisite virtue. The truest essence of these is found in the entire life of Christ, for the scriptures record not one instance where Jesus placed His desires and interests above those of anyone. He took up the cross and was the sacrificial Lamb on Calvary, but daily the world's only innocent man was subject to "like temptations" and daily He always overcame them. It is not enough to make a point of comparison and state that He was tempted just as we all are, for

His temptations went to realms unexplored by any other. Early in His ministry, alone in the desert, Satan pressed hard on the Savior, who by a certain point was dying of thirst and starvation, having gone forty days bereft of water and food. Satan tempted Him with the glories of earthly kingdoms, with miraculous earthly powers and most relevant to the moment, with food and water. The Lamb of God resisted them all.

We are told that Jesus presented Himself a living sacrifice, but He did not wait until the closing days of His earthly sojourn to make this sacrifice. Just being here was a sacrifice which as yet we have no means to fully comprehend. A King who sat on the right hand of God Himself in Heaven surrendered this all to save our souls. No one expressed this sentiment more beautifully than did the apostle Paul:

> "But made Himself of no reputation, and took upon Him the form of a servant, and was made in the likeness of men:
>
> And being found in fashion as a man, He humbled Himself, and became obedient unto death, even the death of the cross."

From our lives each of us know life, good and bad, in this world. All have different, basically unknowingly visions of Heaven, yet our consensus, reinforced by the scriptures, is that Heaven is the place of perfection. Jesus willingly and with love took human form and partook of daily sacrifice, all the while doubtless thinking of His true home in Heaven. The Lamb of God in the purest sense was self-sacrificial.

We are entitled to and should probe the nature and extent of the Lamb's sacrifice. The believer accepts that Jesus sacrificed, albeit temporarily, His throne in Heaven, and that He willingly died a horrid, grotesque death. What else did He sacrifice, and were their elements to this sacrificial life which made His existence unique? In many respects and facets of life all men and women are brothers and sisters in certain desires, pleasures, goals, dreads and fears. Most are so common that they become easily overlooked, and so it was with Christ.

Jesus lived in the ancient world, and we live in what we self-assuredly call "modern times." In most respects we engage in the same activities as did the ancients, even employing the same words and phrases yet with vastly different meanings. An obvious example is the word and the concept of "travel". A non-dictionary definition for which is going from one place to another. In the modern world no destination is safely immune from a visit from a person anywhere on earth. Modern means of automotive, train, ship and airplane provide access to any global point, often within a breathtakingly short span of hours. Even accounting for the miseries and degradations of modern security measures and concerns the extent of travel is often limited only by the traveler's finances. Travel in the ancient world was so far removed from modern means it is astonishing. Except for a sojourn to Egypt when He was an infant and very small child no Biblical reference is found wherein Jesus ever traveled over one hundred miles from His birth. Yet for the three years of His ministry He sacrificed the serenity and comfort of home, and was continually on the road, never seeming to stop in His journeys through Galilee, Samaria and Judea. Except for one storied episode at the end of His life where He rode a donkey, travel was synonymous with physical hardship, as one journeyed over narrow rocky roads and paths, many of which were known for the robbers and highwaymen who could emerge unexpectedly, rob, maim, or worse injury being the fate of the poor traveler. For Christ specifically even stops along the way and reaching the destination itself meant no abatement of hardship. He famously remarked and without a trace of self-pity:

> "The foxes have holes, and the birds of the air have nests; but the Son of man hath not where to lay his head."

Even the most humble had homes, but we may only imagine how often did the Savior Himself spend the night outside sleeping, exposed to the elements. His life, especially those final three years, was a test of physical strain and endurance, and among all His sacrifices this, too, should be remembered.

Indeed, it is the rare person who truly does not care what others think of him. Often remarks are made to the contrary in attempts to impress upon others the toughness or cynicism of the speaker, but the man or woman who is truly heedless of others' opinions is rare indeed. In fact, the disciples of Christ are always encouraged to maintain good reputations and to "be of good report" with others. As a youth and a young man Jesus possessed this in abundance as He "...increased in wisdom and stature, and in favor with God and man." Likely in that Galilean village of Nazareth it would have been difficult to find a disparaging word spoken of Him. Such did not endure, and the innocent Lamb of God became and to this day remains the most hated person who ever lived. What a sacrifice, to go from the right hand of the Father to the most hated of men. Why was such a sacrifice made and how did it come about?

For a time, Jesus obtained fame, celebrity and that most ethereal of human qualities, popularity. Great multitudes gathered to hear Him, the lame, the halt, the diseased and the blind were even brought to Him and successfully made whole. A giant multitude followed Him, and He miraculously fed over five thousand souls. Why would He not be popular? Yet it was all transient, and soon the popular appeal faded, was drained away, and He was left with only the bitter dregs of fierce, fanatical opposition and hatred. The study of the accrual of popularity and that modern phenomenon celebrity is really a separate discipline all to itself. In some, actually many, if not most, instances its source is difficult to define. It may be money, physical attractiveness, political or other types of power, or a combination of all these factors. Jesus possessed none of these, yet He retained a magnetism never seen before or since, and with Him it is not so difficult to envision and define. He gave men and women not just what they needed but what they wanted, both physically and spiritually. It took only a little time, though, before it became evident that His followers were divided into two basic categories. The first, and sadly likely the largest, were those who were in the throng solely for what they could receive from Him. Maybe more free food was on the horizon or perhaps a long-time ailment, injury or disease could be eradicated by His healing touch. For whatever reasons they followed it became clear to them that perhaps being a disciple of this Master would afford some hardships and pitfalls. At the conclusion of the famous feeding of the five thousand Jesus continued with His disciples and reminded them that God had always taken care of His followers and had fed and clothed them. But now He began to speak of food and drink in a seemingly ghoulish and macabre manner. He looked upon them and with wording that must have stunned even the most faithful explained:

> "Except ye eat the flesh of the Son of man, and drink
> His blood, ye have no life in you.
>
> Whoso eateth my flesh, and drinketh my blood, hath
> eternal life; and I will raise him up in the last day."

Was the price of Heaven cannibalism? Such a conclusion is an absurdity, though doubtless many were driven away by hearing such graphic terms. Even more likely is the reality that even more great numbers were repelled by the thoughts that following this man, this great teacher, would actually require something from them. True Christian discipleship would be based upon living a life of substance, and the follower of Jesus would be required to follow a certain path, a pathway requiring real commitment. The refusal to follow this path is still the choice of the vast majority, even the majority of those who hear the truth. The substance of the Savior is too much for most, and they render to no effect the ultimate sacrifices of the Lamb of God. they turn away and to them the blood of the Lamb is wasted and spilled to no effect whatsoever. Any sentient reasoning person realizes the hurt of having done a favor for someone, even to the point of making great sacrifices of time, money and emotion, and having no reward. Those that benefit turn their backs or in extreme cases openly spurn the gift of sacrifice. Few human pains equal this for emotional intensity and devastation, but the sacrifice of Christ was on a scale and dimension far above even the best of humanity. It was the extreme sacrifice of leaving the Throne of Heaven and humbling Himself as a human to receive degradation, debasement and dismissal. All this after the self-sacrificial Lamb of God had offered Himself as "...the Way, the Truth and the Life," the one true way to Heaven and the avoidance of the natural consequences of sin. This He did willingly, not as a conscript, but as a volunteer, a substitute for the life of every man and woman who ever lived. He, though, is "...despised and rejected" and the mass of humanity finds no use for Him or His sacrifice. We must view Him as the Son of Man, a human, and His agonies and tears doubtless have not been confined to that night in Gethsemane two thousand years ago.

Even with Christ it is easy to fall into a pattern of concentrating on the "big" things, the items which we deem to have been the major sacrifices in His life. The humble birth, the denial of any material comfort beyond life's necessities, the embittered organized ferocious opposition of the religious establishment and of important persons are all easily seen and ascertained. Not so often suggested as sacrifice, however, are other matters which in the broad eons of history may be viewed as trivial, but actually are a part of the fabric of the everyday lives of most humans and without which our lives would generally be blander, less fulfilling, less satisfying and not as happy. Nowhere is the sacrifice of the Lamb of God more pronounced and more over-looked than in the vast realm of family. By this is meant not the family into which He was born, for God saw that His Son would have the finest of parents when He chose two obscure Nazarenes, Mary and Joseph, as His earthly mother and father. Even in a world which has vastly changed in the last two or three generations the names of these two still shine brightly and are revered to this day. Mary , the most honored woman in history and rightfully so, and Joseph, unbeknownst to themselves were to be esteemed above all other parents, and it is difficult to see that Jesus was therein shortchanged in any manner. Earlier it was noted that Jesus was the eldest in a family of at least seven children, so it is unlikely that as a child and youth He suffered any deprivations from sibling companionship.

Many will maintain that their lives have proven friendship can be more vital and important than family, and for many persons this is a correct assertion. The Bible itself exclaims "...that there is a friend that sticketh closer than a brother." The Old Testament especially is not shy in reflecting that many of its most famous families were toxic disasters when it came to inter-family relationships, the families of Jacob and David immediately coming to the fore. No wonder, then or

now, that many individuals enjoy more serenity and emotional sustenance with a friend than with a family member. Jesus, blessedly so,
had both, for His character and personality attracted friendship, especially His most trusted disciples, His apostles. But He had others, and
the gospels provide solid evidence that likely His closest friends were
a brother and two sisters, namely Lazarus and especially Martha and
Mary. He was continually invited to dinners, weddings, banquets and
the like, so little sacrificial capital was here spent.

What Christ lacked and wherein His sacrifice was great was in not
having His own family. Any Christian and even the informed non-
believer knows that Jesus had only a short span of earthly years, and
that He came here for a special reason, the salvation of humanity.
He spent that time, though, in the form of a man, and the scriptures
adamantly proclaimed that in all respects He lived as a man, with the
same desires as any other. it should be a desire which almost all humanity can easily and quickly grasp. Although the late twentieth and
early twenty-first centuries have given birth to rapid social changes,
alterations and even destruction of longstanding social structures and
institutions it may be confidently asserted still that the average young
man is attracted to girls and young women. The best of them desire
marriage and seek commitment and the opportunity to create and
build a family. The earliest recognition of this was God Himself in
the early narrative of Genesis where He declares:

"It is not good that the man should be alone."

Yes, the contrarian may aver, but Jesus was the Son of God here
for special reasons, and this was not among them. True enough, but
He was likewise the Son of Man with the same passions as any other
man. The New Testament explicitly states that in all ways Jesus was
tempted in every manner as is any other man, yet He was without sin.

It may be stated categorically that no man in either the Old or New Testaments is described as being in the company of women more than Christ. He was born of a woman who yet today is recognized as the ideal of motherhood and femininity. In His ministry He dealt closely with women of all ages and backgrounds, both Jews and Gentiles, elderly women, little girls, women who were desperately sick or handicapped, women who because of various factors were deplored as vile sinners and the outcasts of society. Even more than men, women seemed to intuitively grasp that this young Master was different.

The Son of Man had a plentiful abundance of personal exchange with many other women, especially those who were His closest disciples, many of whom traveled with He and the apostles and were among His closest friends. The likelihood that these women were all aging maternal and grandmotherly figures is remote. We must recognize without hesitation that Jesus likely saw as many pretty and attractive girls and young women as any man of His time. Further it would be foolish and frankly absurd to believe that He was blind to their attractiveness and did not find it appealing. From Adam forward the rightful appreciation of feminine charm and beauty is one of the prime benefits awaiting men. Yet other men can act upon that desire to move forward with a relationship, a Divinely ordained blessing. Jesus could not and did not. This Son of Man was denied the pleasures, comforts and feminine solace which man has celebrated for millennia. He made friends, taking friendship to heights never reached, could socialize and teach, but the denial of a special relationship burdened the Lamb of God. Jesus expressed in so many ways but none plainer than when He told Zacchaeus that:

> "The Son of Man is come to seek and save that which
> is lost."

His reasons were greater, yet He was still denied the blessings and delights which through the ages have inspired the greatest writers, poets, sculptors, and composers. Yet this part of the sacrifice was not the greatest (wonderful that it is). His special mission, His reason for being here in temporal form meant that He was denied the benefits and comforts of domesticity and the bliss of marriage. In our age of extreme cynicism, where the institution of marriage and even the idea of family itself has become a prime subject of sport and mockery such a phrase as "marital bliss" is automatically a joke to many. It was not to Christ, and at least as a standard has never been so in most societies.

Christ lived without the daily comforts a happy marriage affords a man, a loving wife whose instincts at love and nurturing are usually greater than her husband's, tenderness, comfort and just the ordinary routine pleasures of a simple home. All was denied to the Son of God, who had no permanent dwelling place and literally slept out often in the elements of nature. The old adage is that "A man's home is his castle." Christ, who left the throne of God in Heaven, had no home, no castle, and well was it that He was born in a manger, a harbinger of His humble life to come. We may only speculate at the frequency of making His bed on the hard, stony ground while other men were abed nestled softly and comfortably next to their wives. Even these basic life sustaining pleasures did the Lamb of God forego.

Centered firmly in the Christian's heart is an awareness and a recognition that just being here on this earth for a short span of years was a sacrifice for the Son of God. In fact, it is the foundational sacrifice upon which the entire structure of His lifetime of giving and sacrifice is built. Not once did Jesus show any resentment at being here in the role of a human being, with all the foes which any man faces writ large. We dream, aspire, imagine and fantasize about the nature of Heaven, but Christ knew it as His natural home. For mankind He bore everything and offered Himself a sacrifice as the Lamb of God. Lambs, though, need shepherds, so who is the shepherd?

{ 11 }

THE GOOD SHEPHERD
AS PROTECTOR

The scriptures are replete with mentions of a multitude of trades and occupations, most of which have a modern equivalent and even in some instances being practically identical with their ancient Biblical counterparts. The first and probably still the most vital of all was that of a farmer, a trade first pursued by Adam. Both Testaments are full of stories and parables not only of farmers but also of carpenters, bakers, butlers, maids, vintners, merchants, builders, scholars, teachers, lawyers, doctors, kings, priests, ministers and the list trails away ad infinitum. None is ranked on the scale of importance either above or below any other, and both in context and by teaching all are treated with respect as honorable pursuits. A familiarity with Bible history, Bible stories and even the parabolic teachings of Christ draws one to an inescapable realization that one trade, if not elevated above the others, was at a minimum "first among equals." The Biblical names of the shepherds or those who in some manner were so associated is its own roll call of fame. It begins with Abel, the first murder victim, the great Patriarchs Abraham, Isaac and Jacob, many of Jacob's sons, King David as a youth, a vast number of the prophets, both renown and obscure and into the New Testament those who were first introduced to the birth and nativity of Jesus were shepherds tending their flocks. In Christian teaching the image of a shepherd is perhaps foremost of all occupations. The numbers of artistic depictions of Christ holding a lamb or being nuzzled by a flock of adoring sheep who surround Him as long been commonplace. The Master made endless allusion to sheep and lambs in His teaching, and without the Divine employment of these constant ovine images and metaphors the New Testament would require a major rewriting. All in all, a modern reader is drawn irrevocably down the path leading to the obvious conclusion that the continually highlighted and praised shepherd must have been the most prestigious and honored of professions. Yes, the reader would so be led – to a wrong conclusion. None of these statements is true, for the shepherd by the time of Christ held a low place, a very low rung, on the societal ladder.

A shepherd was actually a voluntary outcast of society. By definition he was a "herder of sheep" which required his constant companionship with his flock, and likely most shepherds, especially the successful ones, became more comfortable in the company of their sheep than with other human society. It was hard, harsh, lonely outside work, requiring never ceasing attention to a flock of basically harmless and basically unintelligent animals, who by their nature and herd instincts were continually skirting the edges of peril and danger. Not only were their days and nights drudgery likely they were comprised partially of protracted periods of boredom. Also, anyone familiar with animals other than the cleanest domestic variety is certainly aware that they possess a natural unpleasantness in their odor, compounded by their herding together in a flock. The aroma doubtless was shared and absorbed by the shepherd and became one of his trademarks. Likely, the most appropriate comparison to the ancient shepherd would be the nineteenth century American cowboy, perhaps the most romanticized figure in our history. An entire genre of literature and entertainment has evolved and been devoted to the idealization of this character, very similar to the manner in which the shepherd has a very positive and potent religious and cultural aura. The reality for each was entirely the opposite. People then and now may have romanticized them, enjoy books and motion pictures which centralize their characters dramatically. They were interesting to read about, talk about, write about but not to be a part of respectable society. So, what did Jesus of Nazareth select as a name, an image, an expression which is the most Biblically comforting of all – the Good Shepherd.

Not only did Jesus identify with the lowly shepherds, but He was also eager to claim the title, using it in self-reference repeatedly. Once when He was teaching, He spoke His most intimate discourse on the nature of a shepherd and His personal commitment to being one as He said:

> "I am the Good Shepherd: the Good Shepherd giveth
> His life for His sheep."

The foundation of Christian doctrine proves that this was more than a mere statement or just a metaphorical teaching device. In the same setting the Master described an intimacy of the shepherd with his flock, an intimacy which Christ took to its zenith:

> "I am the Good Shepherd, and know My sheep and
> am known of mine."

The good shepherd, tending his flock in the field, has to love his sheep to really be good, just as an elder, pastor or minister must love those he tends. Christ expressed such an intimacy to us, His sheep. To most of us, totally unfamiliar with the raising and nurturing a flock of sheep see all sheep alike. One sheep looks the same as another, they smell alike, sound alike and move as a herd all in the same direction. This is not the view of a shepherd, or at least a "good" shepherd, for Christ Himself explained that:

> "...the sheep hear his voice: and he calleth his own
> sheep by name, and leadeth them out."

The sheep are individuals with their own names and the Christian is an individual to Christ, a person possessing a name and fully differentiated from all other sheep in the flock. To our Good Shepherd the lowliest, plainest sheep is as valuable as the flock's prized member. Self-esteem is a huge problem, with many persons, but to Christ, our Good Shepherd, we are all individuals, whose names are not only known but are dear to Him. That Christian, not well known outside her own family and a small circle of friends is as precious to this Shepherd as any who has spent a lifetime of fame in the spotlight or winning the popularity and plaudits of others. If a sheep is in the back of the flock habitually, He is in the fore of Christ's mind. When the Good Shepherd reaches out His staff to guide and protect one of His charges most often it is one who is not in the front rank of the flock, but rather just that, "one of the flock," that is, to all but the one who really matters, the Good Shepherd. To Him there exists no number one, no favorite, no most popular, for no sheep exceeds another in value. For each this Shepherd gave His life and still remits all His love.

It may be difficult to dispute that "love" is perhaps the most ill-defined and the most difficult to define word in the language, any language. Whatever it may be, though, it is best exemplified not by words but by conduct. Truer words have never been spoken than "God is love." It is an indisputable reality, but it is also a cliché which has been worn almost to practical meaningless by overwhelming overuse. What is the nature of this love that for which God is so justly praised and which is exemplified and personified by His Son, the Good Shepherd? It is a love to a degree unknown and incomprehensible by the finite human mind, yet its evidences are not merely abstract and theoretical but real and easily seen and described though not fully understood. In the macabrely comic but strikingly profound book of decades past, The Screwtape Letters, C. S. Lewis drew the irresistibly interesting yet repellant character of Screwtape and his nephew Wormwood. Screwtape is a mid-level bureaucratic servant of Satan, and he has been charged with training young Wormwood in the arts of destroying souls. Wormwood has been assigned the task of corrupting the soul of a young man, and he is experiencing increasing success. Screwtape, though, is wise and warns Wormwood of a weapon possessed by the opposition for which the "Dark Side" possesses no real defense. With malevolence but with hints of fear and envy Screwtape counsels Wormwood:

> "One must face the fact that all the talk about His love for men, and His service being perfect freedom, is not (as one would gladly believe) mere propaganda, but an appalling truth. He really does want to fill the universe with a lot of loathsome little replicas of Himself creatures whose life, on its miniature scale, will be qualitatively like His own, not because He has absorbed them but because their wills freely conform to His.

We want cattle who can finally become food; He wants servants who can finally become sons."

Through fiction (the highest quality fiction) Lewis expressed the ultimate truth that ultimately the Good Shepherd's asset of self-sacrificial love prevails over the predator.

These truths are best seen in the illustrations of vigilance and endurance. The task of a shepherd is what we today call a "24-7" position, for it requires eternal round the clock vigilance. Yes, we are cautioned that Satan is predatory, and as Peter remarked "...he walks about as a roaring lion, seeking who he may devour," but at times he relents. Not every moment of a disciple's life is one of unremitting temptation and pressure, for the Devil and his angels are not omnipotent and omnipresent. In this manner, the contrast with the Good Shepherd is truly stark and comes to us in the brightest of highlighted colors. Carefully and with exquisite detail did Christ describe the Good Shepherd's tending and protection of His sheep, especially as the dark ominous curtains of night lowered on the scene. At night a shepherd would usually gather his sheep in a sheepfold if one was available. Generally, a sheepfold was a stone circular enclosure in which the flock would be herded and the shepherd himself serve as the watching sentinel at the opening, which served as the door. With crystal clarity did Christ describe to His disciples:

> "I am the door; by Me if any man enter in, he shall be saved, and shall go in and out and find pasture. The thief cometh not, but for to steal, and to kill, and to destroy: I am come that they might have life, and that they might have it more abundantly."

None of us are sheep in the literal sense, but the serious minded should find the maximum of comfort in His statements. Fear of night and darkness is inherent in our composition, and likely it never fully departs, no matter how old we may be. The image of reclining at night, safely within the enclosure, with Christ Himself watching for predatory beasts, is a picture of tranquility and serenity hard to equal, much less surpass. Nowhere did Jesus employ the imagery and rhetoric of the Good Shepherd's love and care to greater effect than in these verses. The ideas of love and His special compassionate caring for a disciple, though, permeate every word of His teaching. Towards the end of his life His great apostle and close friend wrote the simple words which to this day inspire the Christian:

"Cast all your care upon Him: for He careth for you."

A text in the Book of Hebrews reflects that He is not only willing to hear our problems but implores us to come to Him:

"Let us therefore come boldly unto the throne of grace, that we obtain mercy, and grace to help in time of need."

The Christian, even the strongest spirit and soul, is likely often hesitant to come to God with certain problems, but the Good Shepherd is imploring us to follow this path. Any mother or father with a normal parental spirit not only wants the child to come to him/her but their hearts at times are begging the children to share problems, fears and temptations with them. How much more so is it with the Good Shepherd. Taking care of anyone, whether a human or a sheep, means dealing with their problems, and as the old hymn spoke "…softly and tenderly Jesus is calling."

In no place and in no conception is the love and care of the Good Shepherd for His sheep more poignantly expressed than in a statement where He is referenced not as a shepherd but as a priest:

> "Wherefore He is able also to save them to the uttermost that come unto God by Him, seeing He ever liveth to make intercession of them."

The true, pure justice of the Father would dictate that all humanity should be condemned, for we are all faulty, and sinful, falling far short of His Glory. Nonetheless, by the redemptive blood of the Savior His disciples are saved, and Divine Wrath is placated through Christ's intercession.

An intercession is simply defined, but in spiritual terms it is monumentally important. An intercessor steps in and acts for another. Christ's greatest intercession was on Calvary where He interceded on our behalf, assumed the place of every man and woman on the cross, and died not for His sins, which did not exist, but for ours. This is at the core of the central truth of Christianity, but the intercession did not halt on Golgotha. The scripture plainly states that He "ever liveth to make intercession." Our intercessor, out Good Shepherd, never ceases. Even the best of mothers and fathers, of loving husbands and wives, cannot give unceasing labor and care for those they love, but Christ will. Each of us knows the problems with which we have had to wrestle, the demons and devils we confronted, the conditions, the illnesses, the heartaches and heartbreaks, the unrequited loves and the ceaseless tramp of difficulties through our lives. Many of these we have confronted, some subdued and some remain unresolved and even worsen until the blackening shades of night engulf us and painfully absorb life, energy and joy from our being. In heed to His call the Christian turns to his Shepherd, his great intercessor for help and at times the help comes to mollify our desires. On other occasions we pray and seek this same intercession from that tender, loving Good Shepherd and ...nothing happens. Our discouragement, our despair deepens, and we almost surrender to the despondency that the difficulty brings, and all the time we should be recalling the phrase "ever liveth." When we have prayed until the words and thoughts cease their flow, when we have with words, deeds, actions, plans and schemes tried every imagined solution to our difficulty, when we can no longer even express our difficulty, when we can no longer even express our oppressive heartache, when every tear has been cried and all we can do is sit and stare blankly into space He still is making intercession for us at the throne of His Father. Not for a scintilla of a second does our intercessor, our Good Shepherd cease caring for us and our problems.

Any person who as a child had a reasonably good upbringing recalls that feeling, the warmth, the indescribable comfort of home when their parents watched over them and all that made life good and worthwhile. Those feelings of home have been described lyrically by so many, whether in prose, poetry or song, and they never fully recede from our minds. Perhaps if we are allotted one word only to describe that feeling and emotion it would be "security." Home is not home unless it is secure, that one locale we know is safe from danger. Christ, the Son of Man, knew home both in Heaven and on earth, and it was He who expressed the certainty of the salvation of His sheep:

> "And I give unto them eternal life; and they shall never perish, neither shall any man pluck them out of my hand.
>
> My Father, which gave them Me, is greater than all; and no man is able to pluck them out of my Father's hand."

The security of the believer has long been a contentious topic within Christendom and has split vast numbers of believers into sectarian positions where unity would otherwise be found. This short essay is not pretentious enough to claim to be dispositive on the issue. Christ, though, is concise enough an His words indicate that no man, woman or other power can force a believer from the sheepfold of protection. The sheep, though, may always voluntarily leave on his own accord and reject the grace and protection of the Good Shepherd.

With ardor and enthusiasm Christ claimed the epithet of the Good Shepherd, and in so doing proclaimed by implication and inference that if a Good Shepherd exists so must His opposite, a bad shepherd. The Savior never showed the least hesitancy in speaking of bad shepherds, describing them, defining and at times even naming them. Who were and are the bad shepherds then and now, by what markings and characteristics are they known and what should be the stance and attitude of the flock towards them? Few knowledgeable persons would confine the concept of a bad shepherd to a Biblical and historical curiosity, for they appear as plentiful now as they were twenty centuries before. Jesus spoke clearly of their traits.

It is revealing that in this lesson on the Good Shepherd from the Gospel of John that Christ most succinctly defines a bad shepherd as a "hireling," its traditional usage denoting one who works primarily or even solely for money. Jesus was aware that when all is going smoothly and with no problems all employees, workers and owners may appear to be performing well and at a high level. Without difficulties and dangers, the performance and character of the good and bad shepherd appear remarkably similar. To Christ we refer the stark yet beautiful explanation of when the distinction comes:

"...the good shepherd giveth his life for the sheep.

> But he that is an hireling, and not the shepherd, whose own the sheep are not, seeth the wolf coming, and leaveth the sheep, and fleeth: and the wolf catcheth them and scattereth the sheep."

By no means is this a condemnation of the majority of humanity that works for a salary or wages. It is a severe rebuke and a revelation of the foul character of anyone who works solely for money to the exclusion of all else. The bad religious shepherd, the numbers of which have always been legion, is often, perhaps more often than for any other reason, tempted into religion, into the Christian world by the enticement of money, maybe even "easy" money. It is no indictment of the many sincere ministers, pastors and teachers to speak openly and clearly on this subject as did Christ. Many who are "shepherding" their flocks are mercenaries and charlatans with no real concern for those who welfare they are to watch. Sadly, but not surprisingly, often when trouble comes to their flocks, they are the primary center of distress. In the modern era of mass media and munificent widespread prosperity it still astonishes when we consider the wealth that certain celebrity evangelists, television hosts of "religious" programs and more traditionally various popes and priests have accumulated. Nowhere do the scriptures or Christ Himself ever condemn wealth per se, but the personal aggrandizement built on the blood of Christ is a sin as scarlet as His blood.

Realistically, though, the above described bad shepherds with multi-millions in net worth are but a few. Some other traits, more importantly perhaps, distinguish the bad from the good. Replete through all Christ's teachings is the theme that the Good shepherd loves his flock. With confidence likewise may we observe that the good shepherd, minister, pastor or teacher is marked by a true love for the fellow Christians he seeks to shepherd, lead or influence. In the plainest language He must love the Church and its members, as the good shepherd, lead or influence. In the plainest language He must love the Church and its members, as the good shepherd does his flock. Clarity of speech and meaning certainly does not fail the Good Shepherd when He spoke sharply of the fraudulent:

"All that ever came before Me are thieves and robbers: but the sheep did not hear them."

The attitudes and words of Christ grate on the modern ear, which has been trained or propagandized to think in terms of diversity and inclusiveness. When it comes to the sole role of the Good Shepherd Christ has proven to be narrow and exclusive. The Good Shepherds do not include Buddha, Mohammed or anyone who maintains that he alone has the Divine imprint of authority to speak and teach. The Good Shepherd is singular and exclusive, Christ and Christ alone.

In the field a shepherd literally is tending to and caring for animals, the nature of this care being more fully explored in the following chapter. In many manners' animals are similar to people, and just as some persons are more attractive to us and pleasing to our sensibilities so it is with animals. In the realm of what we consider the "higher" animals almost all the young are considered especially pleasing and adorable. It is a rare person, a truly curmudgeonly soul, who does not find most puppies, kittens, and here more pointedly to our interest, lambs, to possess an innate adorability which draws us to them. We want to hold them, cuddle their soft fur, talk to them and even treat them as babies. This was and is the easy part of shepherding, and without even considering the multiplicity of problems which the young animals may bring to their owners and keepers, let us ponder the status of attractiveness of the youth when they mature. The good owner, the good shepherd still loves them, but that instantaneous attraction has faded, as the cuteness has eroded and given way to maturity. Little distinction in this regard is to be found with humans, as the cute youngster is not so sparkling anymore. It has long been a universal truth that the young are more likely to be attractive than the older, and so it remains with most. Again, with animals, how many puppies and kittens or even lambs were doted upon and fawned over by owners who were briefly mesmerized by their charms, but as age and maturity had their way the love and doting gone way to indifference and neglect. These traits are not only indicative but also definitive of the bad shepherd. The love of the Good Shepherd only increases with time, and this tender provider realizes that each of His sheep have special individualized concerns and problems that need special attentive care and love, a love that never diminishes.

Continually Christ stressed the permanence of His relationship to His disciples, emphasizing that no matter the nature, extent and stresses that come upon them He was always present. He is the one, the truly Good Shepherd who is ever vigilant, always watching, loving and careful, and it was before His ascension to Heaven that He assured His apostles:

> "I am with you always, even unto the end of the world."

The Good Shepherd's eyes are always upon His sheep, and they are eyes which never close.

{ 12 }

THE GOOD SHEPHERD AS COMFORTER

Likely, it is the most famous poem ever written, endlessly cited, taught, certainly the most quoted, and it was written by a shepherd about a greater shepherd:

> "The Lord is my shepherd; I shall not want.
>
> He maketh me to lie down in green pastures:
> He leadeth me beside the still waters
>
> He restoreth my soul: He leadeth me in the paths of righteousness for His name's sake.
>
> Yea, though I walk through the valley of the shadow of death, I will fear no evil: for thou art with me; thy rod and thy staff they comfort me. Thou preparest a table before me in the presence of

mine enemies; Thou anoinest my head with oil; my
cup runneth over.

Surely goodness and mercy shall follow me all the
days of my life: and I will dwell in the house of the
Lord forever."

Universal familiarity has bred no contempt for these few words of
David's 23rd Psalm, and the haunting beauty of these few phrases,
especially from the King James translation, still comforts troubled
and weary spirits. The author of this Psalm is history's second most
famous shepherd, David, who as a boy and youth lived and worked
in the profession. He thus knew whereof he spoke. Even three thousand years hence and based upon his extensive Biblical record of sin
any observer and reader would conclude that David was a good, even
exemplary, shepherd for his life and work demonstrated his amazing
abilities in all fields. Effectively, though, the subject of this work is
not David himself but rather a man whom he never met but was his
famous descendant, Jesus Christ Himself. We are empty of evidence
that Jesus was ever a shepherd, but He self-identified and Christians
have always attributed to Him the role of the Good Shepherd. Every
phrase and every word in these six short verses in an explanatory
description of the Savior's unique relationship to His sheep, His disciples. As clear and pure as any words penned in either Testament,
the 23rd Psalm demonstrates the nature and extent of the Good
Shepherd's care. They are the words of a spiritually mature disciple
who realizes deeply the extent of the love received from his Shepherd
in all situations, especially those fraught with peril. Every word is
achingly beautiful, and while of a depth of purpose and understanding
unmatched it addresses in simple terms the simple concerns of life. Its
opening phrase synopsizes all this.

Who takes care of me, looks after me, tends to my needs and wants? No one is lacking this concern, and it should be a concern. Entering this world is perilous, and God's natural order is that everyone have parents, a father and especially a mother, the earliest and blessedly to most still the greatest caregiver in life. She shepherds the baby to whom she has given life, and ideally with the companionship of the father shepherds the child through infancy, childhood and youth into adulthood. The fortunate person finds others, perhaps including ministers, pastors, teachers and such who provide degrees of guidance. The ideal marriage reflects husbands and wives seeming to the other spouse's needs and "taking care" of them. That desire, even those who or who proclaim their fierce independence, never really departs a person. The Psalmist David here identifies the one lifelong shepherd as the Lord, a shepherd who provides so fully and amply that His charge "shall not want." That is a heavy burden which the shepherd has assumed, for His sheep need three elements above all, food, water and protection, all of which only the shepherd can provide.

Christ, our Shepherd, has so promised us that David could exclaim "I shall not want" a remarkably, even astonishingly huge burden our Shepherd assumes, because we humans, His disciples, want a lot. As for food and water, the basics of life, their assurance to the disciples is so frequent in the scriptures as to not require additional repetition. We are more than animals, though, and we certainly are not sheep. Our needs and certainly our wants far exceed that of any other creature and rightfully so, for we are the ones made in God's own image. God knows this, and through Christ, and from His own lips He has assured us of our wants. Those comforting assurances fill the pages of the Bible, but symbolically Christ often employed words of the shepherd's idiom:

"It is written, That man shall not live by bread alone,
but by every word of God."

Certainly not by bread alone, but our Shepherd is cognizant of our material needs, but while providing that He answers our deeper spiritual wants. No more clearly, though, did He express commitment to removing want and the resources He offers to any man or woman who seeks meaning and purpose in life beyond materialism than in His conversation at the well with the Samaritan woman. He made a simple comment to the woman that He had a special water, which piqued her interest and desire, as He responded:

"But whosoever drinketh of the water that I give him shall never thirst; but the water that I shall give him shall be in him a well of water springing up into everlasting life."

The Good Shepherd softly yet boldly has proclaimed Himself as all His sheep ever need. No other god, no religion, no philosophy, no political system and certainly no materialism can slake the thirst and fill the soul as does Christ. He is the one Shepherd who truly and completely provides freedom from want.

All have certain traits in common with sheep, and like these creatures we need rest, and not only rest, but comfort solace and serenity, and for this the Good Shepherd offers "green pastures" and "still waters." The twenty-first century citizen certainly needs no special instruction on the importance and prevalence of "green" pastures, for we live, at times with excessive self-confidence and even fanaticism, in an Age of Green. Conservation and beauty in nature are gifts that should be appreciated by all, and their origin is certainly Divine. In a scientific sense, the modern age is the age of greatest and most extensive scientific awareness, but is an appreciation of nature solely the theme of David? Is it even the primary theme of this verse, or does the Shepherd offer more than just green grass, verdant meadows and lush forests dense with trees? Are the "still waters" the result of a lapse of wind and storms, or does their tranquility probe more profound depths.

The modern age is no time of pastoral serenity, and even those souls who wish to resist are likely to be swept along, whether forwards, backwards, or sideways, by the overheated and overstimulated pace of modern living. This is the Age of Busyness, a technological wonderland accelerating at ever-increasing speeds, total, instantaneous communication throughout the entirety of the globe. Step aboard the conveyor of progress and even entertainment but bid farewell to the concepts of serenity, peace and here in the Psalm, pastoral tranquility. Activity, work and energy are never condemned in the scriptures, yet as with all things the Bible frames them in their proportions. A common modern lament which spans the continents and oceans, all races, all nationalities, both men and women, old and young is that "I do not have enough time." Although Jesus lived in the first century His knowledge of this is full and He, the Good Shepherd, is aware of the burdens and weights which even ordinary living carries. He spoke with His voice, but His heart with emotion when He saw our first century ancestors and implored them:

> "Come unto me, all ye that labor and are heavy laden,
> and I will give you rest."

He saw the burdens carried by even the best of His disciples, His dearest friends, and the Good Shepherd wanted them lessened. It was to His close friend, a magnificent and exemplary lady named Martha that He gently soothed her overwrought emotions:

"Martha, Martha, thou art careful and troubled about many things."

In contrast, her younger sister Mary was resting in green pastures and beside still waters, just listening to the Master speak:

"But one thing is needful: and Mary hath chosen that good part, which shall not be taken away from her."

Two thousand years ago even Christ's best and truest disciples needed to be slowed from the pace of life, so how much more we in the frenzy of modern living. It is the Good Shepherd Himself who is the green pastures and the still waters, for He alone provides a peace. Writing in the 400's it was the famous theologian Augustine who exclaimed:

"Our souls were made by Thee and made for Thee, and they find no rest until they rest in Thee."

Neither the Father nor the Son ever promised an earthly life free of troubles, one of mere contentment and pleasure and problem free. They did, though, promise that the disciples would never be abandoned in the thick of battle. Christ, through His great apostle Paul assured us that we could find the "… peace that passeth understanding," a peace that fills the void in every soul. the great seventeenth century mathematician turned theologian Blaise Pascal observed that "… in every human heart is a God shaped vacuum." God longs to fill that vacuum with His Spirit, where we have full access to the green pastures and still waters that "restoreth" our souls.

Several decades ago, American popular culture through its musical airways became acquainted with a song of enormous, though (as with them all) fleeting popularity, a song with the unusual title of "Bridge Over Troubled Waters." The lyrics promised only a bridge, but Christ, the living water, promised that the troubled waters of the soul would be stilled by the Good Shepherd.

Every sentient person who has ever lived has needed the touch of the Good Shepherd, who "restoreth my soul". Not only is this action central to the mission of the Good Shepherd, but also more aptly is it stated that restoring souls is the reason itself for Christ's mission and work. With the early fall of man, the human race became the prey of the Prince of Darkness, Satan. Cast from an Edenic paradise the relationship between God and man had been irretrievably and eternally broken. Humanity had fallen and been revealed as flawed, seemingly incapable of being reconciled and restored to a perfect Creator. It is Christ who has made the path as "… the Way, the Truth and the Life" and provided that needed reconciliation to God, but His role remains immensely more than being the agent of the soul's salvation (as if that alone were not enough). The reconciliation of God and humanity is ultimately fulfilled in Heaven. We remain in this world, though, and the manner in which the Shepherd restores our souls here deserves study.

Sometimes it is a challenge to express certain thoughts without resorting in whole or in part to well-worn clichés', but even so we may concede that even the most over used adages and truisms contain truth, sometimes in large quantities. Only the person totally removed from the rush of daily living and its pressures would fail to recognize that any life is a battle, even a war, in which the participating combatant is not only wounded but repeatedly and continuously wounded. Personal defeats, disappointments, betrayals, losses and even and perhaps especially our own conduct give us wounds of the soul and spirit that alter us, debilitate us and in certain cases make us want to give up.

The Bible is far from a happy compilation of bright cheery narratives where all end smiling and with songs in their hearts. Its readers know that it is many things, and sadness, heartache and depression are never in short supply.

In the Old Testament is found the story of a man whose reputation among the Jewish people was the equal of Moses, a man who synonymized the prophets, Elijah. His miracles, confrontations with Ahab and Jezebel and his life of faithfulness remain beacons in the dark. Yet, he is also remembered for a period of depression, where his body, soul and spirit were so much in despondency that he literally wished death for himself. Days, literally days after the great triumph on Mount Carmel, the defeat and humiliation of the Canaanite priests of Baal, Elijah is hiding in a cave at Mount Horeb, lamenting his fate and wishing his own death. Queen Jezebel has sworn revenge and the life of the prophet Elijah is squarely in her sights. The Shepherd, though, does not chastise Elijah and does not rebuke him, but rather He encourages him, allowing him to rest for forty days before rejoining the fray. God has tasks for him to perform in both Israel and Syria and He has paths down which he must walk, the "paths of righteousness." Elijah, as great a man who ever lived, responds, arises and continues his exemplary walk down these paths, the same lanes in life that the Shepherd has marked for him.

For a moment Elijah had become what we all become so many times and so often in our earthly existence, a "cast sheep." Sheep can be clumsy creatures and often if they fall and roll over on their backs they become "cast" or incapable of righting themselves and getting up without outside assistance. Any shepherd would know of this common ovine frailty, and all spent much of their time righting their sheep and directing them forward. It was the mark of a good shepherd, and is there any save the supremely smug and self-assured who does not recognize how often he has needed such a shepherd's services to align him in the proper path in hos own life. The Good Shepherd is ever there to guide us into those paths of righteousness.

Greater, though, than the time spent in correcting the cast sheep or watching with vigilance over the flock must be the time which the shepherd devotes to finding the lost sheep. The Good Shepherd incessantly made reference to this as His earthly mission and He always stressed that He came to "…seek and save that which is last." Only He fully understood that without His shepherding love every single soul is lost and is fair game for all predators, who serve another power. He lamented with a spiritual paid likely incomprehensible to us when He looked upon Jerusalem at the teeming multitudes of the lost and moaned:

"They are like sheep without a shepherd."

The lifespan of a sheep without a shepherd is of short measure and they are achingly weak without protection and guidance.

The wise, experienced and good shepherd knows that not all of life, even a sheep's is an unending vista of green pastures and beautiful, still waters. The sheep's life is darkened by those same specters which intrude upon the serenity and happiness of all living matter, and whatever forms they may take eventually become the darkness of danger and death. In the blackening skies that roil on the horizon, when fears begin to envelop the flock of sheep as it will the spirits of His disciples the Good Shepherd remains. Likely the most beautiful and comforting sentence ever composed is from the Psalmist as he expresses both danger and solace:

"Yea, though I walk through the valley of the shadow
of death, I will fear no evil: for thou art with me; thy
rod and they staff they comfort me."

Fear and loneliness are so closely related that at certain moments
they are close to impossible to distinguish. An infant or baby reflexively cries when she does not have her mother close at hand, touching
her, speaking softly to her, even if the baby's presumed "desertion"
is but for a moment. An adolescent begins to feel his self-confidence
growing into a demand for independence from parents, until danger threatens, and the comforting touch of a loving father or mother
becomes essential. Even Christ dispatched His disciples and even
the apostles in pairs to they would not be alone and without mutual
support.

Many things threaten death to a sheep. Depending upon the geog-
raphy and topography they included wolves, bears, predatory big cats,
rough terrain, the weather and the sheep's seemingly inborn inepti-
tude. The shadow of death looms large always and continually threatens to become the final curtain of death. The disciple of Christ, too,
seemingly has many predators, traps, temptations, death and soul-de-
stroying situations. Alone depending upon his strength and stamina he
may at times persevere. The real predator, though, the "roaring lion"
of Satan overmatches any single Christian who ever lived. The protection of the Good Shepherd shelters and comforts the disciple through
the endless array of valleys awaiting us in life. Because of Him we are
aware of evil, but now we fear no evil.

The Good Shepherd of the 23rd Psalm does not barely save those
in His charge and care but rather He leads His sheep from the dark
lanes and corridors of death not just to safety but to glorious triumph.
We are assured that He "…preparest a table before me in the presence
of mine enemies." The earthly author of these words was intimately

acquainted with enemies and personal triumph. A one-time shepherd himself he wanted his sheep not just to survive but to flourish. His Biblical debut was his contest with a great enemy of Israel, the Philistine giant Goliath, and David's triumph alone gave him immortality, fame and acclaim only a few years passed, though, before David's triumph was converted into a continuous storm of threatening death from King Saul, the man who promoted the young David (albeit unwillingly), and became essentially mentally deranged from his jealousy of David.

Left to their own devices sheep are not the calmest animals. Neither are they the most intelligent, the most alert, or the most watchful. Sheep, especially herded into a flock, become servants of the mentality of mob thinking and emotion. They easily are frightened, spooked and to employ a cattle analogy of the American West they become frenetic and stampede. In summary they are not the bravest of creatures and require a good shepherd's continuous care and comfort. The good shepherd knows that on a consistent basis what makes life a misery and a burden to his sheep is not the hidden wolf or lion ready to pounce and gobble them up, but rather something which in great numbers drives his flock to a virtual madness. Insects, especially flies, beset sheep, particularly in the warmer months. A sheep will be tormented, irritated and eventually driven to a type of spasmodic frenzy attempting to escape from the swarming of the flies, their endless buzzing and the increasing pain of insect bites. Especially vulnerable is the head region, the eyes, ears and nose, and left to themselves if not destroyed by the insects the animal's life becomes an abyss of hellish misery. Especially in ancient times relief could come only from the Shepherd, for certainly the animal itself was a helpless victim. The ancient remedy was an anointing of a mixture of olive oil and various perfumes and spices, rubbed, caressed and massaged onto the poor animal's head, the remedial effects of which were remarkably rapid and thorough. Whereas moments before the animal was a dervish of uncontrolled frenzy, not knowing when, where or how to find relief it was now becalmed by the soothing touch of the shepherd's hands. The Good Shepherd, and only the Good Shepherd, could so provide.

Only the Christian's Good Shepherd, Christ, provides relief from the frenzy and the ceaselessly accumulating annoyances and pains of life. Guardian of us in the major catastrophes and cataclysms of living His presence may be felt even more in that accretion of anxieties, annoyances and petty problems that are so much a part of the fabric of life. These are the matters which we define in so many fashions but recognize intuitively as the "one thing after another" which can sap from us so much of the joy of life. Our Shepherd knows all about this, He lived among us and experienced it all firsthand. He has already told us and more importantly shown us that He gives His life for us and is ever making intercession for us, endlessly comforting us and anointing us to calm the disciples from the frenzies and fears of life. "My cup runneth over" is the Psalmist's joyous recognition that comfort from Christ is drawn from an inexhaustible reservoir, His love and devotion for His flock. He never tires of providing sustenance, succor and comfort. How mindful this is of Christ's teaching in His famous parable of the Prodigal Son, wherein the extravagantly foolish son has reached rock bottom in a foreign pig sty, humiliated and starving. Then to his beaten soul and battered heart comes the beautiful image of his Father's house, where he knows that "…there is bread enough and to spare." Not just enough to sustain him but an endless plenty to restore him body and soul. So, it is with the touch of the anointing hand of the Good Shepherd, for unlike us He never tires of any of His flock. His love and comfort is not constrained by boundaries or self-imposed limitations.

Like the sheep of the Bible our lifespan here in this world is limited, and in reality, of a shockingly short span, but the Good Shepherd abides here and forever. In Heaven we will truly want not for anything, for the abundance of our needs and even wants we cannot contemplate will be provided, and truly we "... shall not want." The beauties, tranquilities and serenities of ever flowing streams, verdant meadows adorned with flowers too beautiful for our earth will now be commonplace. The souls of the saved will be finally and irrevocably restored by simply being in the presence of the Good Shepherd. Death, evil and darkness will not even be remembered, and their absence is a portion of heaven's definition. Most importantly, though, and most comforting it will never stop and under the Good Shepherd's loving watch we "...will dwell in the house of the Lord forever."

{ 13 }

RESURRECTION AND THE LIFE

Resurrection in the New Testament is a rather commonplace event, and in many instances, while important, is not especially newsworthy or interesting. Also, it is a word which is susceptible to a remarkably simple definition, which in the main the Concise Oxford Dictionary defines as:

> The act or an instance of rising from the dead.

In common English vernacular the word is often employed with a certain casualness and a self-conscious lack of seriousness which often borders on flippancy. For example, a football or basketball team may be moribund for a protracted period of time, but they "catch fire," begin winning and are said to have resurrected the season. A politician's career may have stalled on the way to the top with the re-sume' including two or three consecutive losses, when in an upset he is victorious and praised for resurrecting his career. Actually, though, in such mundane, pedestrian examples no person or other living creature has come back from the dead, but only an athletic season or political career, hardly the substance of miraculous works. The New Testament, literature's storehouse of resurrection events, though, has its pages filled with resurrection stories of far more import. These are resurrection events which are categorized in one of two columns, the resurrection of the body and that of the soul, and in certain instances both. Any with an interest in this subject or even just a passing familiarity with the Christian religion knows the centrality of resurrection to the faith. The belief that Jesus Christ died for our sins, was buried and rose again on the third day is the foundation of Christianity, the truth upon which all is hinged. Jesus spoke often of this event, both prospectively and in retrospect, yet so much of His daily teaching was centered on another type of essential resurrection, the coming to life of a person's soul after being dead to sin.

A common theme begun by Christ, carried forward in apostolic teaching and still essential in Christian theology is that a man or woman living in sin without Christ is dead. Again, we reference the parable of the Prodigal Son with all its despair, ecstatic joy and pathos. The elder brother is furious at his forgiving father who has accepted with warmth and love the return of the erring younger brother, whom the elder views with the greatest contempt. The elder son is so filled with anger and loathing with both father and brother that he is oblivious to what has occurred in from of him. To the elder's son's rage at the banquet given for the younger the father tenderly responds:

> "It was meet that we should make merry, and be glad:
> for thy brother was dead, and is alive again; and was
> lost and is found."

When the younger son returned to the father not only did his mortal person come but more importantly his soul was resurrected from the dead. Fittingly, in this parable, perhaps more than any other place, Christ Himself recognizes that sin can be fun, that there is great mirth and merriment to be found with superficial friendship. Unless the person escapes such fun before it has hardened into habit and character, he finds himself gripped in the cold clutches of the death hands of Satan himself. Yet by coming to himself the younger man's soul and spirit was resurrected.

Honestly, every Christian conversion story in the New Testament is a similar tale of resurrection, and each has its own unique blend of sentiment and inspiration. Most importantly, a soul must be rescued from the dark caverns of sin, but at times sin is not the problem, or at least the only problem. The New Testament writers never showed a reluctance to chronicle the weaknesses and fears of even its greatest figures, none of whom were greater than the twelve men Christ personally chose as His apostles. The history of the Savior's dealing with eleven of these men (we will exclude Judas Iscariot) is a fascinating story in itself. It would be an overstatement to state that their faith waivered at times. More appropriately it was their knowledge and understanding that sometimes failed. All through the Last Supper they are models of befuddlement, not understanding what Jesus means when He says that He is going away and rejecting outright Christ's claims that where He goes no other man can walk. The most outspoken among them, Peter, flatly contradicts Christ and morally boasts that even if all deny Christ, Peter will remain steadfast even to death, and so stated all the other apostles. Yet they all failed Him within hours when He prayed in Gethsemane with His close apostles Peter, James and John lapsing into sleep. He stood along before the high priest, Herod Antipas and Governor Pilate, and His temporary abandonment extended to Peter's denying that he even knew this man Jesus. They then witnessed both the impossible and the most important moment since the Creation, the crucifixion, death and burial of their beloved Savior, a man who they accepted as the Son of God. He was treated worse than the worst criminal, humiliated, beaten, tortured and diabolically transitioned through unimaginable pain, all within the space of a few hours on that Good Friday so long ago. Now these same men, so inspired, so enthused literally hours before were huddled together in an upper room, shaking and shivering not from cold but from fear. If Jesus Christ could be so unjustly accused, condemned and murdered, what of His followers? With much apparent justification they awaited doom. If ever a group of men was defeated and despondent for those two days following the crucifixion it was the apostles. Their identities could not be hidden indefinitely and the next knock on the door could precede an imminent invasion of the Jewish authorities or even more ominously, the Roman soldiers. Instead, the next to appear was one of Christ's closest disciples, Mary Magdalene, who heralded the news that the Savior had appeared and spoken to her. Still, that Sunday evening they remained cowered and fearful in that upper room when no door opened, no knock was heard, but Jesus Himself appeared in the midst of them. Fearful, disbelieving and astonished initially all these emotions changed to rapturous joy with the realization that the Master, though dead, now lived. The hopes, lives, plans and futures of all these men were now resurrected as much as was Jesus when He rose from the grave. Actually, though, it is more accurately and clearly expressed that this is the moment in which the resurrection began. For forty days Christ remained on this earth and while they might not have been continual, He still had dealings with His apostles. The recorded conversations are thorough enough to establish that these men knew that they were disciples of a man who had literally returned from the tomb of death. Their confusion was not entirely abated, though, and upon Christ's ascension they were instructed to return to Jerusalem where once again they assembled in an upper room. Luke's historical account in Acts records in detail their reception of the direct miraculous powers of the Holy Spirit, whereby they were endowed with even greater knowledge of God's desires. Then later that day, the great Jewish holy day of Pentecost, Peter with the other eleven stood in the midst of thousands of assembled Jews and with power and authority told the story of the life of Christ, his passion, burial and resurrection. In answer to the powerful clarion call over three thousand heeded the apostles' message, obeyed and were baptized. The Church had now begun. Are we not almost compelled to make the comparison of the Peter and his denial of Christ and the powerful, confident Peter of Pentecost, and may we not conclude that here, too, was a resurrection that could only be affected through the power of Christ.

It is a good thing for a young man to be intelligent, and it is certainly admirable for him to be diligent, hard working and of a high moral character. When channeled into the right streams and currents it is even honorable for a young man to have ambition. Who would not be proud to be the mother or father of such a son or to claim such a young man as a friend or brother. Both Testaments record several examples of such young men, but the most famous of these makes no Biblical appearance until after Christ and in the Book of Acts. When we first encounter him, though, he was "dead while he liveth" and his soul seemingly beyond the life-giving miracle of Christ. He was the man later known as the "apostle born out of due season" but in his debut as Saul of Tarsus, Christ's and the early Church's greatest persecutor.

The initial review of Saul's background, personality and character may excite many emotions, not the least of which is jealousy. He was a Jew, born in the Cilician city of Tarsus in Asia Minor, modern Turkey. As he later described it Tarsus was "no mean city" and in fact a center of intellectual renown and prestige, having an ancient university, a likely place where young Saul was a student. As a Hellenic Jew Saul was exposed to and absorbed the cultures of both his native Jews and the intellectual and artistic advancements and brilliance of the Greco-Roman world. By his own later admission, he was a Jew's Jew, "a Hebrew of the Hebrews" who had been personally tutored by Gamaliel, the greatest of all Jewish professors. His knowledge of many subjects appeared to be encyclopedic, and his personal moral standards were of the highest grade. Intellectually he was arguably the equal to any man or woman who ever lived.

To the early Christians, though, young Saul of Tarsus was their most deadly foe, a maddened fanatic who

> "...made havoc of the church, entering into every
> house, and hauling men and women into prison."

A leading participant in the persecution and murder of Stephen, the first Christian martyr, even the death of such a man as this did not slake Saul's thirst for blood:

> "And Saul, yet breathing out threatening and slaugh-
> ter against the disciples of the Lord, went down into
> the high priest..."

Went down for what we likely ask? He wished letters of authorization from the high priests to arrest any Christian he might find in Damascus, his next destination.

Saul's resurrection commenced on the famed road to Damascus. Struck down by a light which literally blinds him a heavenly voice confronts him with:

"Saul, Saul, why persecutes thou me."

Now, it was the arrogant, self-assured young man, a man whose name struck fear in the hearts of Christians as the harbinger of misery, persecution and perhaps even death, who was scared. He was scared and effectively speechless (not a common condition for him) as Christ Himself directed that he be led, now blinded, into Damascus where he would be taught by a man named Ananias. So, it went, the persecutor was now the student and the destroyer of Christianity now became one himself as he was baptized. As the Bible often explains he was a "new creature" in Christ, but effectively his personal resurrection had just begun. He was at the beginning of a very long journey, starting with three years in Arabia where he would learn more of Christ and then his return to serve as the most prominent of all the apostles. The man who seemingly hated Christ the most became His most famed evangelist, "the apostle to the Gentiles" and became the most intensely hated man among his Jewish enemies, who at one time had been his supporters and confidantes. From this point the New Testament is essentially the story of Christ as told by the apostle Paul (the new name affixed to Saul), and in his own words Paul glories not save in the cross and is happy to be known as "...a fool for Christ." All those qualities, ambition, intelligence, diligence, even wealth, which Saul of Tarsus had buried in the bosom of his own personal drive and hatred had not died but now had been resurrected and laid at the feet of Christ. History, whether Bible or secular, documents no other moment of such dramatic change, where the old man of sin died to be replaced by a resurrected spirit in the image of Christ. Resurrection is the only correct term.

Peter, Paul and all the apostles with the hosts of Christians through the ages have all experienced the resurrections discussed, although few as dramatically as did the apostles. The Bible, though, is far more than a book of allegories and metaphorical instructions, as it discusses, no "confronts" the idea of resurrection after physical death in the starkest terms. Death is Satan's great gift to the world and to humanity, and its specter hovers over every person from infancy to demise. Its fear rarely departs too far from anyone's thoughts, and our dealings with those fears in large measure define our character. From the Fall of Man to the twenty-first century mankind's questions have always included that posed by Job in the Old Testament so long ago:

"If a man die shall he live again?"

The answer to this question have ever been important to every soul that has drawn breath in this world. A person's view on this issue is often determinative of how he/she lives, their moral standards and the level of happiness and contentment they experience in life. Actually, a strong argument can be forwarded that it determines everything about an individual's life. The Christian's answer to the inquiry is a resounding yes, probably based on many reasons. Personal hope, logical calculation, an understanding that life is not just carnal but spiritual, and on it goes. At this juncture, though, those reasons essentially fall into a realm of conjecture. The substance of Christian belief rests upon the Christian's reality of resurrection, fact to the believer but fantasy to the skeptic. There were many, though, who believed in the resurrection even before it had come to pass.

We have frequently noted that Jesus' closest friends were likely three siblings, Lazarus, Martha and Mary, who lived in Bethany, a town Christ frequently visited. While Jesus was away Lazarus became gravely ill, causing his sisters to send a message to the master to come quickly so that He might heal their brother. To the amazement of His disciples upon receiving the message Jesus did nothing but instead remained where He was. Finally, He bid His disciples to accompany Him as He went to Bethany, but to what purpose? Before leaving for Bethany Jesus spoke plainly:

> "Lazarus is dead.
>
> And I am glad for your sakes that I was not there, to the intent ye may believe; nevertheless, let us go unto him."

They came to Bethany and were met with a scene of abysmal grief, friends and relatives gathered around the surviving sisters Mary and Martha, characteristically each handling grief in a different manner. Mary, the younger one, quiet, contemplative and studious was entirely true to her manner. Many had come to comfort Martha and Mary, but Mary did not really mingle with the sympathetic well-wishers but rather "…sat still in the house." It was Martha, the active doer, the organizer, the take-charge, essential sister who likewise remained true to character. When she heard that Jesus was coming it was not enough for her to patiently wait, for she hurried out to meet Him on the road. Just as true and consistent as ever Martha displays the same self-confidence and nerve she had done before and effectively chastises the Son of God for His seeming lack of interest in her brother's life. Rather than a simple greetings, an act of obeisance or any indication of friendship and love Martha hits Jesus squarely and upbraids Him with these words, a combination of both faith and criticism:

"...If thou hadst been here, my brother had not died."

Then begins a short-constrained interchange which demonstrates that two persons can outwardly agree but simultaneously be in internal conflict. Christ responds with the words of comfort "Thy brother shall rise again." Martha, as true a Christian disciple as the world has seen responds with an agreement and an acknowledgment that much of humanity still rejects:

> "I know that he shall rise again in the resurrection at
> the last day."

The Savior responds with no words of disagreement but rather with likely the closest to a one sentence encapsulation of truth as was ever uttered:

> "I am the resurrection, and the life; he that believeth
> in Me, though he were dead, yet shall he live.
>
> And whosever liveth and believeth in Me shall never
> die. Believest thou this."

Martha quickly agreed and went to speak to her sister Mary, informing her that Jesus wished to see her. Mary quickly arose, ran out to meet Him (for He was still on the road outside Bethany) and fell down at His feet weeping, and as her older sister did greeted Christ with her knowledge that if He had been there earlier Lazarus would not have perished.

Now was the moment for the Savior to demonstrate a resurrection such as the world had never seen. Jesus, the two sisters, His disciples and the townspeople all went to the tomb where the body of Lazarus had lain for four days. Martha, ever the practical one, cautioned Jesus when He directed that the tombstone be rolled away, for she "knew" that the body, four days dead in a hot climate, would already be decayed and putrid. Nonetheless, Christ proceeded and bid the recently deceased with "Lazarus, come forth." The crowd gathered now watched a different sort of miracle authored by the Master who had turned water into wine, healed the desperately ill, given life to dead limbs and cast out demons. At His word they witnessed a man four days dead walk from the tomb resurrected from death unto life. If the curse of death could be lifted at the word of one man, if that great, burdensome weight could be removed from the shoulders of every creature, every man and woman who ever lived, what was beyond the range or the touch or the speech of this Master?

The resurrection of Lazarus was a touchpoint and a flashpoint both for what then began to occur. From that day many believed (for why would you not heed a man who could raise the dead). Ominously, though, all the opposition, the murmuring, the pettiness of His detractors began to coalesce and metastasize into a specific conspiracy designed to murder Jesus Christ. Bluntly in criminal terms, He had to go.

It is so often, so regrettably often, that the second part of the famous declaration of Christ that He is the "Resurrection and the Life" is overlooked. Likely throughout the centuries of Christian history when the disciples have pondered the meaning of the "Life" their thoughts are of eternal life in Heaven, and well they should be for this is the great reward. We must confront a couple of undeniable truths, though, about eternal life. None of us has yet to experience eternity in Heaven, and for that matter the human conception and grasp of the concept of "eternity" is weak itself. Consistent with His other teachings is the realization that by "Life" Christ meant this earthly life as well. He promised us that He came so that we might have life and have it more abundantly. Christ Himself infuses purpose into the lives of all men and women who accept and obey Him. Because of Him life become more than a series of hardships, problems and woes, although they remain plentiful in every life. It now has a purpose, and its purpose was never stated more succinctly or with more sagacity than did the wise writer of Ecclesiastes as he concluded his instructions on life:

> "Let us hear the conclusion of the whole matter: Fear God, and keep His commandments: for this is the whole man."

Christ because He lived a span in human form knew that any life has problems, troubles, pains, agonies, farewells and finally deaths. Because of Him and His life and sacrifice these matters are more than a jumble, greater than some hodgepodge of afflictions and tortures randomly heaped upon every person. Christ does not just promise a life of purpose, meaning and ultimate reward, He guarantees it by having offered His Body in sacrifice as a surety for the promise.

But what of Christ's own resurrection, that event on the first day of the week over two thousand years past, the one that is "the" resurrection.; To the believing Christian it stands as a monumental moment, an historical and spiritual reality that dwarfs in importance any other event in history. It was that event predicted for thousands of years before and proclaimed for thousands of years since that gives meaning and purpose to existence. In the consistent pattern of Christ's life, it was done out of the spotlight, suggesting almost a private affair and publicized to only a few at the outset. In our age of media extravagance which often lapses into madness everything is publicized, talked and speculated about, analyzed, photographed, critiqued ad infinitum. And Christ's Resurrection? Early one Sunday morning several of His disciples came and found an empty tomb. Perplexed, bewildered and likely more than a little scared they pondered what it all meant. Then in the quietness of a garden in the morning one of His closest followers, not an apostle but an otherwise obscure woman Mary Magdalene in the midst of tears inquired of a man who she believed to be the gardener where His body had been taken. the presumed gardener spoke one word 'Mary" and in that instance the prophecies of thousands of years were fulfilled, and believers knew that life had purpose and meaning. Death was still present in the world, but its curse had been removed, as Mary Magdalene gasped her response "…Rabbani! which is to say Master." The emotions of this scene are beyond the ability of any observer and writer to comprehend much less chronicle, but they represent the outpouring of the first awareness of the fulfillment of thousands of years prophecy. Mary rushed away, told Peter and John and then the other apostles, and the world's greatest gift of life began to be made obvious. Death had been conquered.

But did the resurrection of Jesus Christ really happen? If put to a vote of the world's populace most assuredly the answer would be negative. As for the believer, so many, many arguments have been offered over the past two millennia, but this is certainly not the moment for their summary. Let us confine ourselves to a final look at the scriptures themselves. For the forty days between his presumed resurrection and presumed ascension the gospel authors record ten separate instances of Christ appearing to His followers, walking with them, eating with and conversing with them. In total, we are informed, He appeared to approximately five hundred persons, or witnesses we might otherwise describe. For a short period of less than six weeks His appearances, His speech and comings and goings are recorded with a specificity that is so rare as to be otherwise non-existent in ancient history.

No Christian can "prove" the resurrection to the non-believer. In reality, each Christian's acceptance and faith reasons vary from person to person. Finally, though, let us not concentrate so much on Jesus but upon the reactions and behaviors of the men closest to Him, the apostles. The tragic scene of the Passion threw a grim spotlight upon Peter, and he was seen cursing and denying that he even knew the man. The others, save for John, were nowhere to be found. On the third day after these men were huddled together in secret in an upper room "for fear of the Jews." They were bedraggled, beaten and likely man could now envision their own deaths. Yet these are the same men who spoke on Pentecost, began the church in the face of almost diabolical hostility from the Jewish religious establishment, nurtured it and saw it grow through the historically documented ferocious persecution of the Romans to the point where it was observed of them in the Book of Acts:

"These (men) have turned the world upside down."

Something happened back there so long ago.

{ 14 }

ADVOCATE

The role and image of a prosecuting attorney is not necessarily by any measure attractive. To those with a personal interest in the conviction of a criminal defendant he is their champion, the one person who represents their interests, which are tightly woven with the desired conviction of the accused and his having to face justice. Our adversarial legal system is based upon each of two parties having a spokesperson to represent their respective interests. A good and effective prosecutor is knowledgeable of the facts and the law, is well prepared, is professionally and morally bound to honesty and is representative not of his own interests, but that of his client's, presumably society. He is also relentlessly single minded in his fervor to not only accuse but to convict the defendant of the charges which have been laid at his feet. Every action, each word, the smallest gesture, the presumed trivial moments of the defendant's life are placed in the worst possible light, a light that shines intensely upon the accused in the prosecutor's desire to convict him. No credence is given to what may reside in the heart of the accused, the "special circumstances" of his life, his possible good deeds and otherwise virtuous character. Even the best, presumably most altruistic of the defendant's actions are to be thrust under the white-hot searing heat of accusation. If the defendant has spent Christmas Day distributing gifts to poor children, the prosecutor will distort this fact to where it is seen as "cover" or an alibi for a felonious act or criminal conspiracy. For purposes of prosecution and trial nothing the defendant does is good or even explainable, but rather every action is a link in the chain of criminal conduct. Plainly, the prosecutor is not the most attractive character to be found, for in trial and negotiations he may be relentless, hard driving and needlessly abrasive. Still, though, at least in theory he is bound by law and ethics. Whatever his flaws and defects of performance and character he renders a legitimate, even essential, function, of which no society can dispense. Whatever he does, though, good or bad, he is a pale imitation of the Great Prosecutor.

Satan is a presence in the scriptures from Genesis through Revelation, and though long stretches of narrative are without the mention or hint of his name, his sinister specter is ever present. With his presence, in many forms and guises, comes a remarkable consistency of character. The meaning of Satan, the great, powerful but rebellious and fallen angel is "accuser." He is never reluctant to meet all the demands of this nomenclature. In the closing epistle of the New Testament, John describes Satan's fall from grace and from heaven, but cannot describe his destruction. He yet exists, beaten but not yet eradicated, and still malevolent:

> "... for the accuser of our brethren is cast down,
> which accused them before our God night and day."

We all have arrayed against us a cosmic prosecutor who ever accuses us, and likely with great effectiveness. None of us are without moral fractures and fissures in our characters, and we give him great material with which to destroy us before God. Even the best of God's disciples, perhaps especially the best, are accused and defamed without remit. In ancient Old Testament times Job was a man of great material and moral substance and was devoted to His Creator. It is all a sham, said Satan, and he confronted God with an accusation of Job that seemed quite plausible:

"Does Job fear God for naught?

Hast thou not made an hedge about him, and about his house, and about all that he hath on every side?...

But put forth thine hand now, and touch all that he hath, and he will curse thee to thy face."

Until the ending of the world the echoes of Satan's accusation are heard daily in such phrases as "Every man has his price," "Money talks," and 'He who has the gold rules." All this is distilled cynicism and itself a pathetic shadow of the real Accuser, Satan. Satan was wrong, and even though much of Job's life fell apart he remained true to God, just as the early Christians withstood persecution unto death, and in spite of massive opposition yet today many gladly follow God. We would be short-sighted and shockingly foolish, though, in a failure to realize the devil's power. The thought that someone is continuously accusing us before God, misstating our good deeds and intentions and proudly displaying our bad characters is terrifying. We know who we are, and the thought that every moment of our lives is sustenance for Satan and his accusations is indeed a paralyzing realization. Our secret thoughts, our covetous and lustful eyes, our false pretenses and presentations and too often outright immoral conduct are a deep reservoir from which Satan may draw accusations. Are we doomed after all, and do we not feel as Paul did when addressing the Romans:

> "O wretched man that I am! who shall deliver me
> from the body of this death?"

Such a Deliverer not only exists but reigns and has the role not just of our defense attorney but an advocate, a greater, more polished lawyer than Satan and one who has the never ceasing attention of the Father, for as the apostle John softly assured us:

> "My little children, these things write I unto you, that
> ye sin not. And if any man sin, we have an advocate
> with the Father, Jesus Christ, the righteous."

Succinctly stated, the Christian has the better lawyer, the individual who is better at advocacy than His opponent.

We can only imagine the accusations, true and false, regarding our character which Satan levels at our souls. But what of the Christian's Advocate and really, what is advocacy? Typically, and historically well-meaning persons utilize the terms advocate and attorney synonymously. As with many snap explanations, they are and are not. Literally, an attorney is simply an "agent," a representative of another's interest, which most certainly is descriptive of Christ. Yet an attorney (or "lawyer") as an advocate is something much more than this. Any good lawyer understands that advocacy is more than courtroom theatrics and dramatics. Actually, this is but a small portion of even a trial lawyer's practice, but true advocacy is an inherent element in all legal practice. The client's best interests are not only represented, but continually put forward in the best light available. The client has retained the attorney, and he justifiably requires from him the best services possible. Some assignments are easier than others, and perhaps more importantly some clients are easier to represent than others. When the client's position and status on a particular issue or subject are sound and easily demonstrated the advocate's task is ever easier, and he needs no special pleading or argument. The similarities between an earthly advocate and that of the heavenly must be noted.

Christ, sitting on the right hand of His Father, has no difficulty pleading the cause of a Christian when that Christian's conduct has been virtuous, exemplary and in accordance with the principles taught and lived by Christ. If our lives were the template of perfection, we would need no advocate, inasmuch as the lives would radiate nothing but the light of perfection. Yet, most certainly, they are not so. Men and women of the character of Moses, David, Peter and Paul, and even Mary, Jesus's own mother, need advocacy, and if they must be served how can we deny His services. Of Christ, though, of His ways, His mannerisms, the paths of His thoughts, we know what He has revealed to us. Because of our limitations of finite understanding at time we are left with speculation as to the manner in which He practices advocacy for our benefit, our very souls. It is speculation, but it is a speculation that draws us down roads and lanes of understanding, based upon our own lives and experiences.

A lawyer is an advocate, and the fortunate lawyer is blessed with clients who are easy to represent, clients who are legitimate and honest, well-meaning and always striving to do the right thing. It is tempting to state that such clients are few in number, but such an assertion is incorrect for such clients are not few but rather non-existent. A client, just as a Christian, is human, and even when sincerely well-meaning is prone to errors and mistakes. A lawyer's client may not always be on the "right" side of a particular question or dispute. So, what does his counsel do, does he concede the illegitimacy of his client's conduct or claim and surrender the litigation, the dispute, the documentary interpretation to the opposition or to other parties? This is when the real advocate, the good attorney, shows the skills that make him so, and this is when he truly becomes the advocate. In modern parlance the best advocates effectively "internalize" the positions and interests of their clients. This is not to say that the advocate's task is to turn wrong into right but rather to always place his client's position and conduct in the best possible light. When presented with a complication or difficulty the good lawyer certainly does not concede defeat. Most basically, he ponders how the situation cannot only be salvaged but even turned to his client's advantage. Any construction and interpretation of his actions and position will be in the view most favorable to the client. The lawyer so closely identifies with his client's position that it becomes his own, and in advancing the interests of his client he views himself as advancing his own.

We are again reminded of the beloved apostle's consolation that if we sin, we have an advocate with the Father. Not when our performance has been sterling or when our motives are virtuous or when we serve others in a spirit of sacrifice do we need the Advocate, but rather when we miss the mark and sin. The words which pass between the Father and Son are known but to them, but the entire breadth of scripture provides us with more than a snippet of evidence of their relationship. The author of Hebrews explained that "...He ever liveth to make intercession for us." Outright sin can never be transformed into virtue, and sin merits the wrath and punishment of God. His Son, though, continuously without interruption and at all times places our conduct, even the most sinful, in its best context. Easily we can imagine Christ's explaining to God that an improper outburst of temper and the harsh, cutting words that are often its accompaniment has been preceded by untold stress, strain and fatigue. In His intercession He dismisses not the sin, but rather explains the Christian's behavior in the context of the weakness of all humanity.

What of the so-called "little white lies" that almost all tell, even the best of us? Surely the Savior of the world, the Messiah Himself, does not treat with frivolity and flippancy violations of the Ninth Commandment received by Moses of "Thou shalt not bear false witness." Of this all may be assured, for the Christ of the gospels treated all transgressions with a sense of seriousness unmatched by any man or woman. Yet the Savior was also the Son of Man, a man who lived the stress and strain of ordinary life and knew how easy it often is to follow the path of a slight prevarication rather than absolute truth at all times. In other words, the small untruths designed to spare us embarrassments, remove ourselves from uncomfortable dilemmas or maybe even to advance our own cause, even ever so slightly. Again, the sin is neither blessed nor approved, but the sinning Christian retains his Advocate. Because He lived a life in this world, earned a living by the sweat of His brow and regularly dealt with all daily He knows our difficulties and how easily we succumb to temptations. He cares for us, He and His Father are One, His advocacy and intercession are unceasing, and we are forgiven.

Our Advocate is a "people's" lawyer, not a silk-stocking barrister, a Wall Street practitioner or an academic ivory tower professor, all of whom may be gifted, talented and diligent in representing and forwarding their client's interests. He really knows and understands His clientele, for He has been one of them. Capable of expression in the most highly personal terminology "Christ knows what is like to be me." He knows and feels with a Divine intensity we can only imagine how weak and prone to error any of us, His sheep, truly we are. Honest reflection compels the sincere Christian to acknowledge the essentiality of this in saving our souls, for the scriptures are without elasticity in the central issue of our salvation. God so abhors sin that all the saved, the sincere disciples, even the most steadfast Christians must appear before His Judgment sinless and perfect, not partially so and not "almost but not quite" but rather sinless in its purest form. With this awareness we turn inward and wail in agony "Me! Perfect – an impossibility, and I am doomed." On our own merits and lives how true this is for every soul who ever tread the earth, from Abraham, Moses and Elijah to Mary, Joseph and all the apostles. Our lives and our merits, though, are not the measure of eternity, for we have an Advocate. This Advocate presents our case better than any legal practitioner has ever argued, and because of His life and advocacy our sins are not minimized, they are not mostly forgiven nor are they merely rationalized. they cease to exist. Because of the Advocate's life and sacrifice God is able to view His disciples not in the stained and filthy rags of sin but rather through the prism of the glorious Light of the World, His own Son. Because of Him we are not sinners in the vision of the Father but (as another of Christ's appellations would connote), we, the disciples, are as innocent as lambs.

The life and advocacy of Jesus Christ is so powerful and its efficacy so overwhelming that the sins of even the worst of lives may be washed, and continuously washed, away. Yet our natural inquisitiveness prompts us to ask, "Why would He do this for me?" for I have sinned beyond measure. He is not my Advocate because I am paying Him, nor does he present and argue my case because my morality merits His services. He is my advocate because I am His. The love of God and Christ is so magnificently expansive and rich that it transforms the disciple into a soul whom God loves as much as He does His own son. It is a Divine love on a plane which we truly cannot comprehend, yet we can understand the depths of earthly love. The basis of our understanding is in the closest approximation of God's love for us is found in the bond and the love which a parent, most especially a mother, has for her child. Just as Christ knows our character and personality to a degree unfathomable to others a mother knows her child, the child's strengths, flaws, motivations, inclinations and all other facets which compose the whole of a human being. A good mother inevitably sees her child in the best possible moral light. If the child has done wrong, she does not excuse him or even absolve him of unrepentant action, but she does "make allowances" for him, her attitude prompted by her great sacrificial love. Without really being cognizant of such she is always her child's greatest advocate. If a devoted mother or father is capable of being such an advocate how much more so is our heavenly Advocate and Savior.

All advocacy and advocates require a forum for presentation, argument and ultimately adjudication. That most renown for forums has been present since Biblical days, known by both the ancient Greeks and Romans and countless other races, ethnicities and cultures. The English-speaking word traditionally has assumed a justifiably proud stance in pointing to what is called the adversarial system of justice, a method of litigating all manner of disputes, both civil and criminal, in an open courtroom before a qualified and impartial judge. Each litigant has the right to be heard, to present his or her case thoroughly, adhering to an elaborate and historically developed set of procedures, regulations and rules of evidence. Theoretically, at trial all relevant facts, both favorable and unfavorable, are presented for consideration by the judge and an impartial panel of jurors. No lawyer, advocate, judge or litigant would ever reasonably assert that this system at all times and in all places works perfectly. Its personnel range from the excellent, sincere and moral to the uncaring, ignorant and even outright corrupt. Nonetheless, in general it functions well and with an admirable degree of fairness and impartiality. As such, it is in no wise and by no measure even a remote approximation of Heaven's eternal judicial system, which has not even the guise or glimmer of fairness and impartiality.

Being an adversarial system, we naturally should pivot the spotlight to the adversaries, or rather more precisely the advocates of the adversaries. Fittingly and fortunately the apostle Peter described the prosecutor, the accusing plaintiff, as our "adversary, the Devil." He has spent lifetimes blackening, befouling, and besmirching the reputations and characters of all Christian disciples. The slanders and half-truths with which this "father of lies" has barraged the disciples now cease, and Satan is allotted no speaking time, the stage at last silent. The verdicts, the decisions and the judgments have now all been made, the favorable results having been entered into the Book of Life. These occurrences and events are beyond the pale of fairness which is the essence of humanity's comprehension and expectation of an equitable judicial system. One party, the prosecution, is allotted no time to speak, to accuse or to present any form of a case against the accused. The proceedings are now effectively reduced to a forum for two parties, the Advocate and the Judge.

Of course, this Advocate, Jesus Christ, is one and the same as the person described as Wonderful, Counselor and Prince of Peace, who ceaselessly provides all to His disciples, including the ever-present comfort and peace of His mere presence. He is not only the advocate, our lawyer, but the doctor, the ever-present Great Physician whose prescriptions provide soothing balm for the deepest wounds. Our Advocate is the same one who saw no shame or degradation in the assumption of His part of the sacrificial Lamb of God. Our attorney and protector is the Son of Man who gloried and even reveled in being denominated the Good Shepherd, tirelessly and endlessly tending to

His flock's every need. Through Him and His Resurrection we have real life in this world and eternal, Edenic bliss in the next. All this in only one person, the Son of God who now has the Divine court all to Himself, making the case, arguing for not His clients but His brothers and sisters, "heirs and joint heirs" with Him. Yet here this spiritual pinnacle, when the gates and glories of Heaven are opening to the redeemed, we realize the inherent unfairness of redemption and the road to salvation. Our Advocate has spent ages, all our lifetimes, arguing and forwarding our interests before the Father, yet the Father is not now the Judge. As the apostle Matthew has informed all judgment been turned over to the entirely capable hands of the Son, the same Son who has never ceased making intercession for His disciples, who now stand before the Savior, a Savior who is all these persons and more, both the Advocate and the Judge. Satan's hand is now called, and he is defeated and crushed by an Advocate and a Judge who pronounces the final verdict for His disciples – "Because of Me they are innocent, and now they reap the eternal harvest."

> "Come, ye blessed of my Father, inherent the kingdom prepared for you from the foundation of the world."